Praise for *The 4* ...

'David brilliantly demystifies the world of financi.......... .ins essential business companion. Through great everyday examples and plain language, David brings the world of finance to life, banishing many misconceptions. He sets out a simple yet very effective formula for every business leader to engage with and succeed. *The 4 Figure Trick* is highly recommended, particularly if finance is not your natural strength.'

– *Terry Lees, Head of Leadership Development & Learning Events,*
British Retail Consortium

'An excellent guide through the world of finance, full of important information and easy to understand for those of us who need to know financials without having to be an expert.'

– *Keith Mitchell, Partner, Managed Services, Ernst & Young*

'*The 4 Figure Trick* takes the mysticism out of financial management, making finance accessible to everyone. An essential and enjoyable read for everyone in business - from shop floor to the board room.'

– *Jacqueline Shorrocks, Head of Higher Education, Fashion Retail Academy*

'If you have struggled with finance in the past and the many traditional approaches to learning it, you should try this book – it's a revelation. *The 4 Figure Trick* is the perfect book for non-financial managers to really comprehend what matters when assessing a business and to help them make better business decisions. I plan to buy a copy for all of our management team.'

– *Sarah Andrews, HR & Retail Director, Harrods*

'By focussing on just four numbers, *The 4 Figure Trick* really does make the mysterious world of finance accessible. This is a must-read for any non-financial manager.'

– *Damian McGloughlin, CEO, Homebase*

'David has an uncanny knack for creating simplicity out of seemingly endless complexity. Time and again, he is able to describe simple "tricks of the trade" that allow non-accountants to be able to analyse complicated financial statements like a professional.'

– *Jon Noble, Chief Operating Officer, IG Group*

'David Meckin has produced a thoroughly readable and instructive book which de-mystifies finance. *The 4 Figure Trick* provides its readers with a thorough and simple run-through of the main principles of finance and financial analysis. I recommend this book for all current and aspirant business leaders. Given the ongoing turbulence and pace of change for all size of companies, financial savvy has never been more important.'

– *Dominic Schofield, Managing Partner Board & CEO Practice, Korn Ferry*

'This book provides an accessible insight into one of the most important knowledge areas for anyone working in any business or organisation. Any manager in business will improve their confidence in measuring financial performance and their potential to make the right impact.'
— *Michael Nathan, Associate Director - Emerging Talent Lead, Mace Group*

'*The 4 Figure Trick* is genuinely both interesting and useful for those of us who stand outside the gates of the finance department. If you feel the urge to doze off, recoil or even flee at the sight of management accounts, then this book is for you. I cannot overemphasize how engaging David is as a writer – he does for finance what Bill Bryson has done for science.'
— *Sonia Chesaux, Director of Learning & Development EMEA, Ralph Lauren*

'*The 4 Figure Trick* is a perfect read for anyone who wants to understand corporate and business finance in jargon-free language. I found this book to be quite an eye opener, and David really shows you how simple finance can be. As someone who is not necessarily "finance savvy", I can't recommend the book enough!'
— *Amy Prendergast, Director of Change, People and Learning, retailTRUST*

'*The 4 Figure Trick* is a remarkably straightforward tool to help every manager assess the drivers of profitability within any business, and it demonstrates how different levers can be pulled to improve the outcome. David helps to demystify many financial concepts with his clear step-by step-approach, giving managers across all functions a greater depth of understanding and the confidence to ask the right questions.'
— *Suzanne Harlow, CEO, RSL Awards*

'David Meckin has a gift for explaining complicated things simply. *The 4 Figure Trick* is deceptively simple to read, but it gives financial and non-financial managers alike an unbeatable insight into how to profitably manage a company (or invest in it).'
— *Keith Anderson, Head of the Accounting and Finance Group, University of York*

'I meet so many people who don't reach their potential because of a limiting, inaccurate belief: "I am no good at numbers". Don't be that person! Let David blow away the mystery, show you the beautiful simplicity of numbers, and leave you feeling confident that you can hold your own with the accountants.'
— *Fraser Longden, Chief Operations Officer, Wickes*

'This book is packed with relatable anecdotes and simple explanations that make the language of finance and accounting accessible to non-financial managers. It is a must for executives, managers and emerging talent in every organisation and should be on the reading list of business studies students everywhere.'
— *Marion Kneale, Senior Manager of Leadership and Development, Yorkshire Building Society*

The 4 Figure Trick

David Meckin

The 4 Figure Trick

How to deliver financial success in business
with just 4 numbers

David Meckin

NICHOLAS BREALEY
PUBLISHING

London · Boston

First published by Nicholas Brealey Publishing in 2021
An imprint of John Murray Press
A division of Hodder & Stoughton Ltd,
An Hachette UK company

This paperback edition published in 2022

2

Author photo © Shaaron Meckin
Illustrations by Alena Dostalova

A CIP catalogue record for this title is available from the British Library

Paperback ISBN 9781529343724
eBook ISBN 9781529343731
Trade Paperback ISBN 9781529343717

Typeset by KnowledgeWorks Global Ltd.

Printed and bound in Great Britain by Clays Ltd, Elcograf S.p.A.

John Murray Press policy is to use papers that are natural, renewable and recyclable products
and made from wood grown in sustainable forests. The logging and manufacturing processes
are expected to conform to the environmental regulations of the country of origin.

John Murray Press
Carmelite House
50 Victoria Embankment
London EC4Y 0DZ

Nicholas Brealey Publishing
Hachette Book Group
Market Place, Center 53, State Street
Boston, MA 02109, USA

www.nicholasbrealey.com

To my family, a constant source of joy and inspiration.

Contents

About the Author

© Shaaron Meckin

David Meckin is founder and managing director of Insight Financial Consulting. Previously, he held several senior management positions up to and including that of chief financial officer of a multinational business, working with companies in the United Kingdom, Europe, North America and Asia. He is a Fellow of the Association of Chartered Certified Accountants, a Fellow of the Chartered Institute of Bankers and a Fellow of the Chartered Management Institute.

Over the years, David has developed a reputation for 'turning complexity into simplicity' and making the world of finance interesting, easy to understand and even fun! He regularly delivers management workshops and presents at conferences to audiences from around the globe. He also coaches senior executives in a variety of organizations and is regularly called upon to assess the business and financial acumen of prospective CEOs. Clients, past and present, include numerous FTSE 100 and FTSE 250 companies, along with many leading international brands.

In addition to regular mountaineering trips, David enjoys a variety of activities including flying (he is a qualified pilot) and adventure travel, and is a keen landscape photographer.

CHAPTER 1

Keep It Simple

• • •

'Imagine you're presented with the annual report of a company. It doesn't matter which company; it can be any company of your choosing. There are two things you should note. First of all, there's the length. A typical report can range from just a handful of pages to a hundred pages or more. Second, there are the numbers. Regardless of the length of the report, one thing you can be certain of is that there are going to be lots of numbers – maybe hundreds, maybe thousands. That's a great deal of information to take in. I am about to show you how, in under one minute, you can ascertain whether this business is a success or not. In addition, I am going to demonstrate how, in less than five minutes, you can identify all its core strengths and weaknesses.'

I regularly present to audiences from all over the globe on financial management and this is an opening I often use. Something I always notice, as soon as I say this, is that delegates start to sit up. It's as if I have just announced I am going to prove cows can fly! In a way, though, I have for many people made a statement which appears equally implausible. I've intimated that financial management isn't difficult. Surely that can't be true?

Finance tends to get a bad press, and to a certain degree that reputation is deserved. Many finance professionals have a knack for making the topic seem well beyond the grasp of the average person on the street. Ask most people what they think of when they hear the word 'finance' and the response will often be vast tables of numbers, spreadsheets, inexplicable charts and complex formulae, all washed down with swathes of unintelligible jargon. Indeed, it's often argued a great cure for insomnia is to attend a presentation by a chief financial officer reviewing the latest set of trading results. It will always involve a PowerPoint presentation, and it will always be packed with numbers. Audiences typically begin to drift off halfway through the second slide, and only the most determined can still keep their eyes open by the end of the third.

As we shall discover, the 4 figure trick turns the popular view of finance on its head. It says effective financial management isn't about getting engrossed in lots of detail: it's all about focusing on just a few core figures. Knowing what these figures are and, most importantly, understanding how to manage them, is the key to running a financially successful business.

Before going any further, I need to take you on a journey; a journey I embarked upon that spanned several years. What follows is an evolution of thinking. The 4 figure trick isn't something that miraculously came to me overnight. I am going to walk you through the early days of my career. Not because you will find it a riveting read, waiting in eager anticipation as you turn over to the next page, but because it highlights many of the challenges that exist within modern-day financial management. It's only by appreciating what these challenges are that you will be able to fully exploit the opportunities that will be made available to you through the 4 figure trick approach.

When I went to university in the dim and distant past, I spent three years studying economics, and it seemed like a natural progression at the time to move on into the world of finance. I progressed through a variety of roles, eventually working my way up to that of chief financial officer of a multinational business. Something I noticed along the way, regardless of the company I was working for, was that there appeared to be this enormous void between the finance function – who were busy producing lots of reports – and the rest of the management population who were busy making lots of business decisions. What was particularly worrying was that this phenomenon appeared to be commonplace in many businesses.

What was creating this void? It seemed to all come down to communication. Finance teams were generating lots of information, but the management teams didn't understand it. But it was worse than that. Finance managers love detail – the more the better – whereas most non-financial managers hate detail. So here we had lots of detail being produced for an audience that didn't want or even understand it. Not surprisingly, given the choice, many managers would avoid the world of finance wherever possible. The trouble is, finance is the very lifeblood of business.

A significant part of my role when I was a chief financial officer was trying to break down these communication barriers and engage the general management population in the financial performance of the business. Indeed, it was this aspect of the job that inspired me to set up my own management consultancy. I wanted to inspire managers in other companies to engage with the world of finance and help them make sound financial decisions; but setting up a new business throws up an immediate challenge. To attract clients I would need a USP – a unique selling proposition that would differentiate my business from the competitors.

At the time there were already many consultancies offering courses targeted at non-financial managers, parading such exciting titles as 'Finance for Non-Financial Managers' and 'Introduction to Finance'. It was almost guaranteed that if you attended one of these courses they would walk you line by line through a financial report and explain what each and every line meant. They might even throw in a few financial metrics to spice things up a bit. In fairness, while on the course, you might well begin to grasp the principles being present-ed. The problem is that most managers don't generally tend to spend much of their day studying accounts, so all this understanding gradu-ally dissipates until eventually it's just a distant memory. What's the ultimate impact upon business performance? Nil. Indeed, a frequent comment I've encountered from delegates attending one of my pres-entations is, 'I attended a finance course a few years ago, but I don't remember any of it'.

Clearly, a different approach to educating non-financial managers in the world of finance was required. But what should this approach be? To answer this question required that I go back to absolute basics.

What is the role of a manager? Regardless of the business, the role of a manager is to coordinate and manage resources, whether these re-sources be people, machinery or property. It doesn't matter what func-tion you operate within, whether it be human resources, production, sales, information technology or some other function, you're there to manage resources, which means by definition you're impacting upon business performance. Every decision you make, right down to the length of coffee breaks, can have financial consequences.

This provided me with my USP. Unlike many financial management and training consultancies at the time, I decided at the outset I was not going to teach managers about finance. Instead, I would show managers how they could enhance financial performance through the decisions they made. I wanted to provide managers with a skill set they could apply on a day-to-day basis; something they wouldn't forget. That was the premise on which I set up my consultancy all those years ago.

This was a valuable learning point for me. Managers don't want to understand all the intricacies of finance, but they do want to ensure they're making financially sound decisions. This approach clearly had appeal because, within a couple of years, the consultancy had built up a significant client base – but I had another even more valuable lesson to learn.

Inevitably, when commissioning work, every client had specific financial issues it wanted to address and messages it wanted to communicate to its management population. As a result, I made the decision that the content of all engagements should be tailored to meet these specific needs. At the time, this struck me as eminently reasonable: adjust the messages to reflect operations within the client organization. However, as time progressed, a variety of experiences led me to doubt whether this approach was indeed the most effective.

One experience – fairly early on in my new-found career – involved sitting down with a regional manager for a major retail outfit. The company had just installed a new management information system and this individual was clearly very proud of it.

'Dave, name a product line', he said.

'White shirts.'

'Now pick a date in the last 12 months.'

'12 February.'

'Now name a time.'

'10 am.'

'Now name another time.'

'2 pm.'

'Dave, watch this.'

With a quick press of an enter key, a report appeared on the computer screen, analysing by store the sales of white shirts on 12 February that took place between 10 am and 2 pm.

'Look, Dave', said a now very excitable regional manager. 'You can see what each shirt cost us, what we sold it for, any discounts that were applied and also the profit made on each sale!'

It was at this juncture I raised the inevitable question. 'This is all very impressive, but how does this help you manage your business?' There was a long pause at this point. If this was a movie, you probably could have enhanced the atmosphere by having a few tumbleweeds blowing through the office in the background. It was a classic example of providing lots of information without any consideration as to how it could help improve decision making: lots of figures but no management.

This observation was reinforced more dramatically only a few months later. I was working with a client who was managing a diverse portfolio of discrete businesses ranging from distribution to gaming. My brief was to deliver a series of workshops to the general management population, focusing on practical initiatives that could be implemented to enhance commercial performance. At the time I was aware this client had also called in a global management consultancy to conduct an in-depth strategic review of the entire group. It was while this was taking place that I was asked whether I could extend my current brief to include a few extra days with the senior management team. When I was initially told what the nature of these additional days would comprise, I was baffled.

'Dave, we would like you to take an active role in the ongoing strategic review and we would like you to sit in on the update presentations.'

'I'm confused. You're already paying a small fortune to a global consulting group to conduct this review. Why on earth do you want me to sit in on their presentations?'

'To be honest, Dave, we haven't got a clue what they're talking about! We would like you to join us in these meetings, at the end of which you can sit down with our senior management team and explain what the consultants are saying.'

And that is exactly what happened. I would sit in on the presentations, take notes and later in the day would sit down with the senior management team to demystify the presentation. This was a bizarre situation. Here we have a well-respected client hiring a consultant to explain what another group of consultants are trying to tell them!

Even though I was dealing with the senior management team, all this group really wanted was some clarity. They wanted some clear easy-to-understand messages regarding the strategic direction the group should be pursuing. The detailed multicoloured graphs and charts were all very entertaining, but that wasn't what this senior management team wanted. They were looking for solutions: not heaps of analyses. Once again, lots of figures but no management.

The problem was, and still is, that many finance departments are obsessed with producing reports that are awash with figures. A common comment I have received from accountants is: 'The Devil is in the detail.' I've lost track of the number of monthly board packs I've encountered which laughingly are supposed to 'summarize' trading activity over the preceding four weeks; and I couldn't help noticing that some of these so-called summaries contained over ten thousand figures. This just made no sense at all. Not even the most experienced and astute chief financial officer could digest that level of detail.

The justification I always received was the same: information is key. The general consensus seemed to be that all managers need is information, and that if they get the information, they can use this to make sound decisions. This is why almost every organization is awash with what is called management information. In my experience, the problem is that far too much emphasis tends to be placed on information and not enough on management; simply bombarding managers with numbers will do nothing to help improve business performance. One of the reasons there tend to be so many numbers is they are often used to perform three very distinct functions.

Making decisions in a vacuum is a pointless exercise: there needs to be direction, and this is contingent on there being a clear objective. This is the first key role of figures: *numbers can provide tangible, quantifiable objectives*. Having an objective is of no use if you've no idea when you've reached it. Numbers can provide clarity.

Numbers don't just exist to provide goals to work towards, though. A second extremely important function is to provide information that will aid decision making. A real power of figures is the ability to summarize activity. If I work in a car dealership and during the week I sell 20 cars, I don't need to detail every individual sale to assess how the week has gone – all I need is a total weekly sales figure. One number has managed to summarize my entire week's activity; and reviewing weekly sales performance figures can prove invaluable when it comes to planning sales activity for the future. This is the second role of numbers in business – *numbers can aid decision making*.

Unfortunately, decisions that are made don't always produce the desired outcomes. It's at this stage that some form of feedback is required. There needs to be a system for monitoring outcomes, and this introduces the third function of numbers. Just as numbers can be used to summarize data that is relevant to decisions about to made, *numbers can also be used to summarize the outcomes of decisions already made.*

This suggests, if numbers perform three different functions, then surely three different sets of numbers will be required to satisfy each of these functions. Indeed, in many businesses this is the case. The annual objectives of a business are often encapsulated within some form of medium to long-term strategic plan. To aid in day-to-day decision-making, managers will often be provided with detailed budget reports highlighting areas where performance is deviating from expectations and thereby highlighting where action is required. Then, when it comes to assessing year-to-date performance, there will often be a monthly executive pack. The problem is, each of these documents will typically contain hundreds and, in some instances, thousands of figures. Do managers study all of these numbers? Of course not. So, if people aren't looking at the numbers, why do businesses insist on producing them?

As alluded to earlier, the problem is that too much emphasis is placed on information and not enough on management. Indeed, the more I looked into this phenomenon, the more evident it became that there tends to be an inverse relationship between volume of data and effective decision making. The fewer the numbers, the better the decisions. This isn't a theory – it's a fact.

Here's a quick challenge. What can you glean from the following two numbers?

14,703   18,604

The most obvious conclusion to draw, and what would invariably be the first thing most people notice, is that the right-hand number is greater than the left-hand number. I'm providing you with just two numbers, and I can predict, with reasonable accuracy, what conclusion you will draw.

Now, what can you glean from the following nine numbers?

8,703	9,414	6,338
2,473	7,444	7,676
1,228	8,381	9,006

Maybe you noticed that the first row is the only row which doesn't ascend in value from left to right. Maybe you noticed that the numbers in the left-hand column are in descending order. Maybe you noticed that the numbers in the right-hand column are in ascending order. Indeed, there are a vast array of observations you could make. So here we are with just nine numbers, and already I have no idea what conclusions you're going to draw. Imagine being presented with a set of trading results containing literally hundreds of numbers. It's little wonder most managers don't like figures.

What can we deduce from this? When there are only a few numbers involved, the conclusions to be drawn are obvious, but when there is a vast array of numbers, the messages can become far more varied and confused. Regrettably, confusion can adversely affect business. In its most extreme form it can result in management paralysis, with managers becoming totally unable to make any significant decisions at all. Even if decisions are made, having huge amounts of data to fight through and digest will certainly slow down the decision-making process, which in turn creates its own problems. If it's taking longer to make decisions, this means there's less time to consider alternative (and possibly more lucrative) opportunities. Furthermore, prolonging the decision-making cycle can result in missing profitable opportunities. Probably the most worrying aspect of creating confusion is that it can result in poor, and sometimes even disastrous, business decisions.

This got me to think about my current business model. It was all very well focusing on how managers could make financially sound business decisions, but another opportunity was now presenting itself: an opportunity that could have significant impact on how managers interact with the world of financial management. As mentioned previously, up until this point – whenever I was engaged by a new client – my approach had always been the same: to tailor the content of my presentations and workshops to reflect operations within the organization. This meant, before ever presenting to an audience, there would be a period of research, and this was no easy task. Every business had its own perspective on what constituted effective financial management.

In addition to this, most had their own unique way of structuring their trading accounts, accompanied by their own unique suite of financial terminology. Even deciding how profit should be measured varied enormously from one business to another.

I had allowed myself to be drawn in by these variations in approach without really questioning the rationale underpinning them. The search was on. There had to be an alternative, more effective way to approach financial management. Further research was clearly required. I spoke to directors, senior executives and managers at all levels in a wide variety of industries. Probably the most revealing question I would ask was: 'Of all the numbers you see within your business, which do you regard as the most important?' I could probably have filled several pages with the diverse answers that ensued. Clearly, there was something fundamentally wrong with financial management in its current state. Managers were being bombarded with numbers, and yet they couldn't even identify which numbers were the most important. This can have serious consequences when it comes to business decision making. Two managers could be presented with exactly the same trading report, but one might be looking at how to increase sales while the other might be focusing their attention on how to reduce payroll.

I also ploughed through the annual reports of companies from all over the globe in an attempt to find out why some were succeeding and why others were failing. What became apparent very early on was that success or failure was not being driven by detail. No company was succeeding because it had cancelled the end-of-year staff party, and no company was failing because it had overspent by $700 on the stationery budget. Companies were failing because they had expanded operations too quickly, and companies were succeeding because they had a lean and efficient cost base. This provided a lesson that has underpinned all the work I have done with clients subsequently – the fate of a business is determined by fundamentals, not details. As we've already seen, details can create confusion: fundamentals create clarity.

Looking back over previous assignments, what also became evident was that the underlying principles were the same in every business. It didn't matter if it was an oil exploration company, a telecommunications group, a bank, an insurance business or even a film studio, the financial challenges and the levers available to improve performance were always the same.

If business performance is driven by fundamentals, it follows there ought to be some key measures that track those fundamentals. What I began to realize was that every business can be condensed down to just four figures. It doesn't matter what sector the business trades within, these four figures are key. It doesn't matter if you're setting targets, making decisions or reviewing trading performance: everything rotates around these four numbers.

This unique way of viewing business finance deserved a title. The one I came up with many years ago, and have used in my presentations ever since, is 'the 4 figure trick'. Don't be tempted to think the word 'trick' implies I'm trying to mislead anyone. That's a completely different branch of finance called creative accounting – which is well outside the scope of this book!

The reason I've adopted the word 'trick' is because, when I present the 4 figure trick to audiences, I often elicit a similar response to what I would have expected if I had just performed a mind-boggling illusion. For many managers it's a revelation. That isn't to say I have introduced something that is so ground-breaking it's going to change the world. What I have managed to do, though, is demonstrate that sound financial management is not about wading through copious reports, metrics and graphs. It's simply about managing four numbers. Get this right and you've got yourself a successful business.

This approach to financial management is probably more relevant now than it has ever been. Technology has changed the world and how we work. Nearly everything you need to know is just a click away. What's the current temperature in Nairobi? How long does it take to drive from Berlin to Prague? How do you cook the perfect steak? These are questions we want answered, and we want the answers right now: no delays. We're adjusting to a world where fast is at the heart of everything we do. You have a question? You Google the answer because you want the answer – fast. You want to order a set of headphones. You place your order online because you want delivery – fast. You want to watch a film? You don't wait until it's on television – you stream it because then you get to see it without the waiting. This constant need to have wants satisfied immediately is impacting upon business. It used to be the case that if you had a good business model that was delivering robust sales you were set for life. I remember many years ago working for a bank and being told by one of the senior managers, 'Dave, unless someone makes one almighty cock-up, this business will always make money!' That was in the days when, for many, jobs were for life. You joined a company, worked your way up through the ranks and retired on a handsome pension. Those days are long gone.

Nowadays, if businesses want to survive, they have to constantly evolve. If you don't evolve, you'll die – it's as simple as that – but evolving demands continuous decision making. Companies need to be able to respond to a constantly changing environment. Having time to reflect on decisions before ultimately making them is a luxury most managers can't afford these days. This is where the 4 figure trick comes into its own. By focusing on just four figures, managers

- Are able to assess performance of their business – fast
- Are able to assess the impact of proposed actions – fast
- Are able to review a wide variety of strategic options – fast
- Are able to respond to changing circumstances – fast.

In addition, managers

- Have clarity in terms of commercial objectives
- Feel less fearful of finance
- Feel more engaged in the profit-making process
- Feel more confident when proposing management strategies.

In essence, the 4 figure trick provides managers with the necessary insight and understanding to make better, faster business decisions. The principle underpinning this approach is that numbers should aid decision making, not hinder it.

The philosophy in a nutshell is: if managers focus their attention on these four key numbers and how their actions are impacting upon them, this should result in a better-managed and more successful business. This isn't about sitting down and wading through endless reports. It's not even about being aware of what the current values of the four figures are. This is about being continually aware of what actions can improve performance. In essence, it's about developing the most important skill set there is in the world of finance – having the ability to distinguish between what constitutes a good financial decision and what constitutes a bad financial decision, and being able to do this in a time-effective manner.

How to spot a good   *and*   How to spot a bad
financial decision – fast   financial decision – fast

THE 4 FIGURE TRICK IS ABOUT DEVELOPING ONE SKILL SET

If you want to ensure managers are consistently making sound business decisions, any initiative that's introduced to achieve this goal needs to satisfy four conditions:

1. *It has to engage the managers.*	This means, for it to deliver long-term benefits, it must be relevant every working day.
2. *There must be consistency.*	A common complaint from many managers is that the senior executive team keeps changing the goalposts. This not only causes confusion but it can also prove to be a strong demotivator. What is the point of doing something only to be told the following day you should be doing something else?
3. *It needs to be simple.*	Managers have a myriad of challenges to address every day: burdening them with more complexity can only hinder the decision-making process.
4. *It has impact.*	Any resultant decisions must be seen to be benefiting the business.

One of the big attractions of the 4 figure trick is that it is easy for managers to engage with because, as we shall discover, regardless of their role, every manager affects at least one of these figures every working day. Also, these four figures never change, so there is never a problem with shifting priorities. Furthermore, because there are only four figures involved, it keeps things simple: there is no complex analysis required. Finally, focusing attention on just four figures aids, rather than hinders, the decision-making process.

At this stage, I'm rather hoping I've whetted your appetite and you're keen to know what these four figures are. Before that can be done, though, there are a few principles we need to get out of the way first.

CHAPTER 2

Measuring Financial Success

• • •

This chapter is all about objectives: understanding why businesses exist and what they're trying to achieve. At the outset we need to be quite clear about what we mean by business. A typical definition of the word 'business' as found in a dictionary is 'the activity of buying and selling goods and services'. The key word here is *activity* – business is something you do. Any entity which indulges in both buying and selling can be regarded as a business. If you buy and sell pottery, you're in business. If you buy and sell second-hand cars, you're in business. It's the presence of both buying and selling activities that makes it a business.

Suppose you want to set up your own business. Your first challenge, before you do anything else, is to decide what sort of trading entity you want to be. Most managers around the globe work for companies, and, as a result, for the rest of this book we're going to assume you work for a company. However, to fully appreciate the significance of this assumption, you need to understand the other forms of trading entity that are available. So, before going any further, we're going to take a small diversion into the world of trading entities of which there are three main types available: sole trader, partnership and limited company. Let's look at each one in turn.

The most basic type of trading entity is the sole trader. There are no formalities when it comes to setting up as a sole trader. As with all types of business, you will need to maintain books of account, but, outside of that, there's not much else you need to do. The only other requirement in most countries is needing to submit some form of accounts to the tax authorities at the end of each trading year to settle any taxes due. When you're a sole trader, *you* are the business. You decide what to buy and what to sell. You can even employ people to assist you if you so wish. Legally, though, you're the business, and, as such, this means you're personally liable for the debts of that business. Should the unthinkable happen – your business collapses owing money – you'll be personally responsible for those debts. The attraction then of being a sole trader is that it's a very simple entity to set up, but the downside is that you're personally liable for all of its debts.

An alternative to being a sole trader is to set up as a partnership, which is where two or more of you decide to go into business together. The only real legal requirement in this circumstance is to draw up a partnership agreement which will define issues such as personal rights and responsibilities, how profits are to be distributed and such like. As with a sole trader, books of account need to be maintained and some form of accounts may need to be submitted to the tax authorities to assess the liabilities of the various partners to tax. Just as with a sole trader, the partners are personally liable for any debts the business may run up: but it gets worse. It's common in a partnership for the partners to all be jointly responsible for the debts of the business. In other words, each partner accepts personal responsibility for all the debts the business may run up. Suppose you enter into a partnership with two colleagues and the business ends up heavily in debt, but your two colleagues have absconded and are nowhere to be found. This is very bad news for you because the creditors of the business (that is to say, the people who are owed money) can pursue you personally for all of the debts. So, if ever you consider going into a partnership, be very careful who you choose to be your partners. To avoid this situation arising, some countries permit the creation of partnerships where the personal liability of those concerned is constrained, but there can be significant regional variations regarding what partners are liable for within such an entity.

As can be seen, the big downside to being a sole trader or creating a partnership is the issue of personal liability. It's not unheard of for people to lose their homes in this situation: a high price to pay for setting up a business. Wouldn't it be wonderful if you could set up a business where you're not personally liable for its debts? Welcome to the world of the limited company. Unlike sole traders and partnerships, a company is viewed as a separate legal entity from its owners. This is very good news for you because it means that if the company runs up debts that it's unable to pay, you're not personally responsible for those debts. The people who lose out in this instance aren't the owners; it's the people who the business owes the money to. This explains why companies are such a popular trading entity: the liability of the investors is *limited* to the money they've already invested.

Setting up a company is a bit more complicated than setting up as a sole trader or creating a partnership. The most significant difference is how you invest money in it. In the case of a sole trader or a partnership, you simply open a business bank account and pay your investment into the account. Companies are different because they're regarded as completely separate legal entities from their owners. As a result, investing cash in a company is a bit like making a purchase in a shop. You wouldn't walk into a store, hand the sales assistant $100 and be prepared to walk out empty-handed: you'll want something in return. It's no different when investing in a company. When you invest cash in a company you'll want something in return, and what you receive are shares in that business. So what's a share? A share normally entitles you to two things: part ownership of the company along with a share of its profits. Suppose a company wants to raise $100,000 and to do this it issues 100 shares at $1,000 each. If you buy one share, you'll be the proud owner of 1 per cent of the company and, as such, be entitled to 1 per cent of the profits it makes; if you buy two shares, you'll be the proud owner of 2 per cent of the company and, as such, you'll be entitled to 2 per cent of the profits; and so on.

Quite often, sole traders are very small businesses sometimes comprising just the owner, or maybe the owner and a handful of employees. Partnerships – because there are always at least two owners – tend to be slightly bigger concerns. However, nearly every major business (in order to limit the liability of its owners) will be set up as a company.

So why have we embarked on this diversion into the world of trading entities? From a financial management perspective, there's one very important difference between companies and the other two trading entities we've looked at. In the case of sole traders and partnerships, the owners are the business. No distinction is made between the people who own the business and the business itself. For example, if you set up as a sole trader providing painting and decorating services, you are the business – without you no painting or decorating would be done. Companies are different.

In a company, the people who own the business may not be the same people who run it on a day-to-day basis. Why is this important? It's important because it can create conflict. What managers think is a good business decision may not coincide with what the shareholders think is a good business decision. To be a successful business demands the alignment of these two trains of thought: there needs to be consistency between the managers and the owners in terms of what are deemed to be good and what are deemed to be bad business decisions.

Such a potential source of conflict rarely exists in the case of a sole trader or a partnership: the owners and the managers tend to be one and the same. That doesn't mean sole traders and partners always make good decisions. It simply means that when decisions are made, there isn't somebody else who could potentially lose out if it turns out to be a bad decision. If you're a sole trader or a partner and you make a good decision, it's you who benefits; if you make a bad decision, it's you who loses out. That isn't the case when it comes to companies. Managers make the decisions, but it's the shareholders who will benefit or lose out. A very important feature of the 4 figure trick is to get managers to think like shareholders, thereby avoiding this potential conflict of interest.

What we're talking about here is managerial alignment. A group of managers who may all be excellent in their own fields are of no use if they're all following different agendas, as the result will inevitably be chaos. To be effective, it's essential they're working together as a coherent unit with a clear goal. It's not uncommon in business to hear the mantra, 'We've got to increase sales', only to be replaced a couple of months later with, 'We've got to cut costs'. Then the battle cry is 'We need to restructure'. Next thing you hear is there's a merger in the offing; then there's talk of a takeover; then there's outsourcing being considered; followed by a need to centralize key functions. It's no wonder managers get confused. In this environment an oft-quoted piece of advice is, 'Just keep your head down and hope for the best!' This is hardly an environment conducive to commercial success.

The most significant problem with not having a clear objective is that managerial decisions, no matter how sound they may appear at the time, can have disastrous consequences. I was once called in to work with a client that had seen a significant downturn in sales. The irony was that this downturn was totally avoidable: it was a breakdown in communication that had created the situation. The board of directors believed there was an opportunity to widen the gap between what they paid for their products and what they sold them for. If this could be exploited, it would increase profits. Their logic was that the product managers were being too lenient when it came to negotiating prices with suppliers: a tougher negotiating stance would reduce these costs. It was therefore agreed that for the following year product managers would receive a bonus if they could widen the gap between what they paid for products and what they sold them for. What could possibly go wrong?

When the bonus plan came down to the product managers, they viewed the objective somewhat differently. Their logic ran as follows: we're being charged with the task of widening the gap between what we pay out to suppliers and what we earn from customers. Now that may well seem, at first sight, to be totally consistent with what the directors wanted to achieve. Regrettably for the directors, and the company overall, the product managers spotted an alternative means of widening the gap. Instead of negotiating harder with suppliers to secure better buying-in prices (which could be quite hard work), they came up with the bright idea of increasing the selling prices. Problem solved! This meant they would still achieve the goal of widening the gap and, most importantly, they would get their annual bonus. And that's exactly what happened. Sales plummeted, but the product managers still got their bonuses because they achieved the goal that was set for them.

What can we learn from this tale? The overriding message here is that there needs to be a clear universal objective: everyone should be striving to achieve the same goal. It was quite apparent that in this instance the two groups involved were pursuing very different agendas. The directors viewed success in terms of corporate profits, while the product managers viewed success in terms of the gap between buying-in prices and selling prices. As is often the case in these situations, the company ended up paying the price for a lack of consistency – instead of going up, corporate profits went down.

The most straightforward – and indeed the most effective – way of achieving managerial alignment is to ensure everyone has a clear view of the corporate objective: it's the objective that binds them together. Without an objective, strategy is useless. However, having an objective on its own is pointless unless you have some way of knowing when you've achieved it. Consequently, directly linked to the corporate objective, there needs to be a consistent measure of success throughout the business: no variations; no deviations.

Incidentally, although we're going to assume we're dealing with companies for the rest of this book, the financial principles we'll be addressing apply equally well to sole traders and partnerships.

So what is the ultimate objective of business? Answering this question isn't as straightforward as might at first appear because, for an objective to be effective, it needs to be well defined. You can always spot an ineffective objective because it will be a question grabber. That's to say, the very nature of the objective raises immediate questions. 'We want to be a commercial success'. What do we mean by commercial success? 'We want to be the number one provider in our market'. What's our market? 'We want to be the number one choice for our customers'. Who are our customers? These all sound like reasonable goals to strive for, but they're not effective objectives because they lack clarity. This is where numbers come to the fore. The beauty of numbers is they provide definition – they're measurable. It's very clear whether or not a numerical target has been achieved, and this explains why numbers are so popular in business.

Ideally, then, we're looking for an objective that can be expressed in numerical terms; to identify this, we need to ask a question – why do companies exist? When a company is created, shareholders invest cash in exchange for shares. Why are they prepared to do this? The answer is, for the same reason you personally might be tempted to buy shares in a company or maybe open a savings account. They want to earn a return on their investment: they want the company to make them a profit. In fact, what shareholders *really* want is for the company to make them as much profit as possible. If it fails to achieve what is deemed to be a satisfactory level of profit, the shareholders will either close the business down or sell it off.

We've now introduced an incredibly important piece of financial jargon – profit – and it's probably the most used piece of financial jargon there is in business. But now we hit a very real problem. In my experience, profit is a term that is regularly quoted but much misunderstood. Quite often, when I run management workshops, very early on I will present delegates with a simple problem. I will introduce them to an individual with a hot-dog stand who, during the course of a month, conducts just four transactions. All the delegates have to do is work out how much profit or loss the business has made during that period. I have lost track of the number of different answers I have encountered over the years. What's particularly interesting is fewer than one in 20 delegates ever comes up with the right answer. If the tens of thousands of managers I've presented to over the years is a fair representation of the total management population, this suggests 95 per cent of managers don't actually know what profit is. Indeed, I've encountered main board directors who don't know what profit is; so let's make sure we do.

By the way – this isn't a failing of the managers: it's simply a reflection of the fact that nobody has taken the time out to sit down with them and explain what the term actually means.

At its most basic level, profit is an easy concept to grasp. Shareholders invest a pile of money in a company in the hope that it will turn that pile of money into a larger one. Profit simply measures how much bigger the pile of money is that the company ends up with compared with the pile of money it started off with. Now consider this scenario. Shareholders invest $1 million cash in a company at the start of the year. At the end of the year the company has $400,000 cash, it owns equipment worth $500,000 and it has inventory valued at $300,000. Has the company made a profit? The first thing most people will note is that there is now less cash in the business: it started off with $1 million, but has only $400,000 left. This is where the confusion kicks in. Many managers equate profit with cash. In reality, profit has nothing to do with cash. Profit measures changes in wealth. In this instance, at the end of the year the company may only have $400,000 cash left but it also owns equipment worth $500,000 and inventory worth $300,000. If it doesn't have any debts, that means the company is now worth $1.2 million. Even though cash has fallen (in theory at least) the shareholders could sell the company right now and expect to receive back $1.2 million for their efforts; that's $200,000 more than it started off with. To put it another way, it has just made a profit of $200,000.

What did we own
at the start of the year?

What do we own
at the end of the year?

PROFIT MEASURES CHANGES IN WEALTH

Don't underestimate what we've just discovered here. Shareholders are motivated by wealth, not cash. The easiest way to grasp this is at a personal level. You're presented with two choices: you can put $100,000 cash in a savings account right now and receive back $102,000 cash in one year's time, or you can invest the cash in a property which is expected to be worth $110,000 in one year's time. If you're like most people, you would probably opt for the property deal. Even though you won't be ending up with more cash, what you do have is a property that could be turned into $110,000 cash if ever you decided to sell it. This is a powerful motive for people investing in property, because in many countries property increases in value faster than money invested in savings accounts. All shareholders want to hear is, 'You're richer!'

Now we're in a position to be far clearer about the role of managers in business. Contrary to popular belief, their role isn't to increase sales or to cut costs: the role of a manager is to help create wealth. Increasing sales and reducing costs may assist in achieving this goal, but there are many occasions where this isn't the case.

I was once dealing with a client where the senior management team were obsessed with sales. Their view was that healthy sales will always produce healthy profits. It was a challenging time for the company, so, to stimulate sales, significant discounts were being offered to customers. Unfortunately, this meant that, for many of the products on offer, the cost of the product exceeded the revenue being generated from the sale. Sales did go up, but profits plummeted. This company had got itself into the rather unfortunate situation where sales were actually reducing wealth, not increasing it. The management's response? We're losing money: we need more sales! Eventually, the penny did drop and the company did the smartest thing it had done in years: it stopped doing the unprofitable sales. Sales went down, but profits went up.

On the flip side, I've also worked with companies that are obsessed with costs. To be more precise, they're obsessed with reducing costs. I remember dealing with one particular retailer that was very concerned with its expenditure on payroll. So much so, it imposed a recruitment freeze: there were to be no new hires. This was in October. Two months later, the Christmas rush was on, and the recruitment freeze was still in place. The view of management was still, 'We must contain payroll costs'. I remember walking into one of their stores and seeing huge queues for the tills (bear in mind they weren't permitted to take on any more staff). Then I witnessed the worst thing that could possibly happen in any store. I saw people leaving the queue and putting the merchandise back on the shelves. This is a retailer that had customers who wanted to buy its products but, due to its distorted view of cost management, was prepared to lose the sales. It doesn't get much worse than that. In case you're wondering, this particular retailer went bankrupt three years later, all because it focused on costs rather than wealth creation. This is a classic example of a company that should have spent more on payroll, not less.

There's another really big problem with companies that are obsessed with cutting costs, and regrettably this is all too common. Where the message is continually, 'We must cut costs', this suggests that spending money is a bad thing, and that can promote a culture where managers are always looking for ways to avoid spending. Ironically, some of the most successful companies in the world are those that spend the most money. Spending money is an essential prerequisite to generating profit. Managers should be looking for ways to spend money, not avoid it. There is, of course, a caveat. Managers should be looking for ways to spend money that will ultimately help the business generate more profit. It isn't how much you spend that's important; it's how you spend it that matters.

What we've now established is the fundamental principle that underpins every financially successful business. Business isn't about driving up sales no matter what, nor is it about continually driving down costs: it's about generating profit and creating wealth. Yes, there are many instances where increasing sales will indeed increase profit, and, yes, there are many instances where reducing costs can have a similar impact. What managers need to also be aware of is that sometimes reducing sales can increase profit and sometimes increasing costs can also increase profit.

There was one client I was working with that had appointed a new chief executive officer. One of the first things he did was to change the bonus scheme. Previously, managers were bonused on sales performance. In one of his opening addresses he instructed the management team to forget about sales and focus purely on profit. That simple message radically altered the culture of the business, and within a year profits had increased significantly.

Based on what has been said so far, it may well appear the objective of business and, by implication, the objective of management must surely be to maximize profit. Regrettably, real life isn't quite that straightforward. It's time to look at how to measure financial success.

For the time being, let's keep it simple, and examine the most basic type of investment there is – a savings account with a bank. It really doesn't get any simpler than that. Now suppose you've got two such accounts: one account earned you $100 interest last year while the other earned you $200. Which account is performing better? The problem is, unless you know how much you have invested in each account, it's impossible to say. Suppose you had $2,000 invested in the first account and $100,000 in the second. Earning $100 interest on a $2,000 investment provides you with a 5 per cent rate of return, while earning $200 interest on a $100,000 investment equates to a rate of return of just 0.2 per cent. Even though the first account delivers less interest, it's delivering the higher rate of return on every dollar invested, and this is what attracts investors. The point to note is that financial success in this instance is being determined by the rate of interest being achieved, not the amount of interest being earned.

The same principle applies to companies. I get very frustrated when companies simply announce how much profit they've made. How can you possibly say a company earning $100 million is doing well or doing badly if you have no idea how much the shareholders had to invest to achieve that profit? What we've just established is that profit on its own is not a measure of commercial success. Financial success is all about delivering a healthy rate of return on funds invested. It follows that the objective of a company is to maximize profit as a percentage of the shareholders' funds invested in the business. The role of every manager, from a financial perspective, is to help ensure that every dollar invested in their business is delivering a healthy rate of return. Regardless of whether you work in sales, production, distribution, marketing, human resources, information technology or whatever, that's the goal.

Not surprisingly, there's a measure that examines the profit being achieved relative to the value of shareholders' funds, but, before we look at the measure itself, we need to be quite clear about what we mean by profit in this context, and also what we mean by 'shareholders' funds'.

There are many different profit measures encountered in business such as gross profit, trading profit, operating profit, EBIT, EBITDA, underlying profit, pre-tax profit and so the list goes on. Don't worry if these all look like gibberish: for the purpose of the 4 figure trick, you don't need to understand all of these terms, anyway. From a shareholder's perspective, there's only one profit figure that's worthy of note and it's called net profit (also sometimes referred to as net income or profit after tax). 'Gross', in the world of finance, means before deduction while 'net' means after deduction. Net profit refers to the profit a company makes after paying all its expenses, including paying any tax due to the government. It's a bit like your payslip. Your gross pay (before any deductions) is of interest, but the critical number from your point of view is the net pay figure – the money you've made after paying taxes to the government – because that's your money which you can do with as you see fit. The same principle applies to shareholders. The company can talk about any profit figure it likes, but what counts for shareholders is the profit that's left over after paying taxes to the government. This is shareholders' money which they can do with as they please.

It's not uncommon for companies to try to deflect attention away from the net profit figure. For example, a company might try to dazzle shareholders by announcing a 10 per cent increase in annual operating profit but, if the net profit figure indicates a loss has been made, there's no getting away from the fact that shareholders' wealth has gone down. That's the reality of the situation, regardless of what happens to other reported profit figures.

The only other figure we need to be clear on is what is meant by the term 'shareholders' funds'. There are two ways a shareholder can invest funds in a business. First of all, there's the original investment. This is the money shareholders physically invest in the company in exchange for shares. But there's another way shareholders can invest funds. When a company declares a profit at the end of the year, there are two basic alternatives available as to what can be done with this money. The company could pay the money out to shareholders. This is called a dividend, and it literally involves the company paying cash into the shareholders' bank accounts. The alternative is to reinvest it, but why would shareholders be happy for this to happen? It's a bit like having a savings account. When you earn interest you can either withdraw it – that's what a company would call a dividend – or you might decide to leave it in the account so you can earn more interest next year. Exactly the same choice confronts shareholders each year. When a profit is declared, they can either withdraw it as a dividend or reinvest it so the company can make more profit next year. By the way – it's important to realize that this choice ultimately resides with the shareholders, not the directors of the company.

Unless otherwise agreed, companies are obliged to have a meeting of shareholders each year to review recent performance, present plans for the future and to vote on any proposed resolutions. One very important resolution will often be, 'We, the directors of the company, recommend a dividend of $x on each share'. Then it goes to the vote because the shareholders own the company, and so the final decision must reside with them.

So, when we talk about shareholders' funds invested in a company, we're referring to the monies originally invested in the company in exchange for shares, plus any profits that have subsequently been reinvested. Returning to our analogy with a savings account, if you happen to have one, the current balance is the sum of the money you physically put into the account plus any interest that you have left in the account. Exactly the same principle applies to shareholders' funds.

There's one further minor technicality we need to get out of the way. If I told you I earned $100 on a savings account last year, you wouldn't ask me, 'How much was in the account on 31 December?' What you would want to know is the average balance in the account during the year, because then you can readily establish the rate of return. It's no different when looking at a company. When looking at the rate of return it's achieving, we're interested in the net profit being achieved during the year as a percentage of the average value of the shareholders' investment during that same year.

Now we're in a position to provide a well-defined measure of corporate financial performance, and it will probably come as no surprise that it has a very flashy title – it's called *return on equity*. Return is just another word for profit, while equity refers to the owners' stake in the business (just like having equity in a house). So here it is – the definitive measure of financial performance:

$$\textbf{Return on equity} = \frac{\text{Net profit}}{\text{Average shareholders' funds}} \times 100\%$$

If during a year a company makes $100,000 profit on an average shareholders' investment of $2 million, the return on equity is 5 per cent.

This measure highlights the two most important figures in business: profit and shareholders' funds. In essence, return on equity is summarizing a process: a process which starts when shareholders invest money and finishes when the management declares a profit has been made. This is in stark contrast to managers who are told business is all about increasing sales and cutting costs. Sometimes the most profitable thing you can do is reduce sales and increase costs. It's no wonder so many companies struggle to make money.

One criticism I often hear regarding return on equity is that it's totally focused on delivering a return to shareholders. What about the other stakeholders in the business such as customers, employees and suppliers? Surely, we should be taking their needs into consideration as well. Ironically, the only way you can consistently deliver a healthy return on shareholders' funds is by keeping all the other stakeholders in the business happy as well. It's interesting to note that a reason often cited for businesses failing to deliver a healthy return on equity is failure to maintain customer focus. To keep delivering healthy profits you need to keep your customers happy, maintain an engaged and motivated workforce and have sound, stable working relationships with your suppliers and other relevant stakeholders. Shareholders may provide the finance, but without customers, employees, suppliers, and so forth, there is no business.

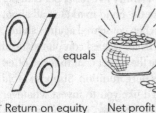 equals as a percentage of

Return on equity   Net profit   Shareholders' funds

RETURN ON EQUITY IS THE ULTIMATE MEASURE OF FINANCIAL PERFORMANCE

Having introduced the concept of return on equity, this immediately begs a question. What is deemed a reasonable annual rate of return on shareholders' funds? I have been in many boardrooms around the globe, and there's a commonly quoted minimum rate – it's 10 per cent. Five per cent just isn't good enough; three per cent is dreadful; and if you're achieving only one per cent, you shouldn't even bother turning up at work. So, why 10 per cent? To understand where this figure comes from, you need to consider what alternatives are available to investors outside of shares. For most investors, the logical alternative is the bond market. This needs explanation.

Governments and companies often need to borrow money. The amounts involved can be substantial, and this can create a problem. Suppose a company needs to borrow $100 million for the next 20 years. One way to raise the funds would be to negotiate a straightforward loan. However, there are few organizations that would be willing to consider lending such a substantial sum for that length of time. An alternative way to raise the money is to break up the loan into individual bonds of, say, $1,000 each. A bond is a tradable instrument whereby the organization that is borrowing the money promises to pay the owner of the bond interest over a predetermined period of time, with full repayment of the amount borrowed taking place at the end of the term. The key word here is tradable – bonds can be bought and sold. As a result, when you buy a bond, you always have the option to sell it to another investor if you need access to cash. Also, because organizations like to be able to plan their financial commitments, it's common practice to fix the rate of interest payable on a bond at the outset.

Many studies have been carried out into the long-term returns achievable in the bond market, and many identify five to six per cent per annum as a reasonable yardstick. Because the bond market is all about loans, it's generally regarded as low risk when compared against shares. As a result, in order to attract shareholders, it's argued companies need to at least double this rate of return: hence the 10 per cent that's so often quoted. By the way – this isn't science, it's pure intuition. Suppose I told you I'm setting up a new business and I'd like you to invest whatever spare cash you may have available. I have to warn you, though, that this is business, so if things go awry you could end up losing the whole lot; but if things go well I'll pay you one per cent above your current savings rate. How would you feel about that? Not impressed, I'm sure. But if I said I can at the very least double your rate of return – maybe even treble it – now it gets thinking space. And that's the logic of the corporate market. If a company can't at least double the rate of return achievable on lower-risk investments, why would anybody be prepared to assume the risk?

Now we're gaining some insight into how to identify a successful company. Is it earning a return on equity of at least 10 per cent? It should be emphasized that many companies regard this as a minimum. Indeed, a study of the major stock markets around the globe over the past few years indicates that by far the majority of companies achieve a return on equity significantly above 10 per cent. Of course, circumstances may alter in the future. However, in a global financial market that has been characterized by low interest rates for many years now, 10 per cent has established itself as a popular benchmark.

In closing, this chapter is important for two reasons. First of all, it has introduced us to the key measure of corporate financial performance – return on equity. Second, it has introduced us to two of the four numbers that comprise the 4 figure trick – net profit and average shareholders' funds. As we shall discover, the 4 figure trick provides the interface between these numbers – it will literally show us how to turn shareholders' funds into profit.

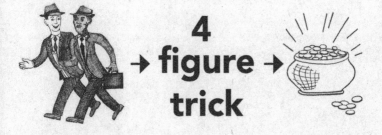

Shareholders' funds   Net profit

DELIVERING HEALTHY PROFITS

Before delving into the 4 figure trick any further, we need to develop an appreciation of the figures that businesses regularly report, both internally to their managers and externally to their shareholders. This forms the content of the next chapter.

CHAPTER 3

Making Sense of Trading Data

• • •

Having invested cash in a company, it's not surprising that shareholders will be keen to receive periodic updates on how the business is performing. To assist in this, every company is required to produce a document each year called the annual report, which is officially a report to the shareholders. In essence it's saying, 'You've given us your money. Let's show you what we've done with it'. Everything managers do during the year is summarized in this document: the outcome of every decision they've made is encapsulated within it. It's only by studying the annual report that shareholders can determine whether or not management is doing what they want them to do.

It follows that the annual report should be answering questions that shareholders would like addressed. So what would shareholders like to know? We've already established that what motivates shareholders isn't the amount of profit a company is earning. What they're interested in is the rate of return being achieved on the funds they've invested, and we've already established that the measure used to assess how effectively this is being done is called return on equity, where

$$\textbf{Return on equity} = \frac{\text{Net profit}}{\text{Average shareholders' funds}} \times 100\%$$

To identify the return on equity of a company, two questions clearly need to be addressed at the outset. How much have shareholders got invested? How much profit has the company made? However, something else we noted in the previous chapter is that profit measures changes in wealth – and wealth is not the same as cash.

It's quite possible for wealth to increase while cash is going down. If you buy a house and the value of the house increases, it follows that your wealth is increasing, but that doesn't mean you necessarily have more cash. The problem is, companies need cash to pay their bills. Even if their wealth is increasing, if they run out of cash, the game is over: the company won't be able to pay its bills, and this will inevitably result in the cessation of trading. Logic therefore says there's a third question shareholders will want addressed: is the company generating enough cash to meet its financial commitments?

To answer each of these three questions, you will typically find within an annual report three financial statements:

1. The *balance sheet* answers the question: How much have shareholders got invested in the business?

2. The *income statement* answers the question: How much profit has the company made?

3. The *cash flow statement* answers the question: Is the company generating enough cash to meet its financial commitments?

Balance sheet

Income statement

Cash flow statement

AN ANNUAL REPORT TYPICALLY CONTAINS THREE KEY
FINANCIAL STATEMENTS

The first two of these financial statements are intrinsically linked to each other. The balance sheet is literally a statement of wealth. It tells you how much shareholders currently have tied up in the business. The role of the income statement (sometimes also referred to as the profit and loss account) is to say whether the wealth of shareholders, as stated in the balance sheet, is going up or going down. When a company says it has made a profit, it's telling shareholders that their wealth has increased – shareholders like to hear that. That's why a loss is such bad news – it's literally telling shareholders that their wealth is going down! The cash flow statement, by contrast, is simply a sanity check that's used to ensure the business can continue to meet its financial commitments.

It's worth noting that interest in these financial statements isn't just limited to shareholders. There can be many other interested parties such as banks, suppliers, customers, tax authorities and prospective investors. For the purpose of the 4 figure trick, our interest in these statements is threefold:

1. In addition to producing the annual report, companies produce regular financial reports for internal use by their managers. Understanding these three key financial statements in the annual report will greatly aid in the interpretation of internal management reports.

2. Most companies love to use financial jargon, much of which emanates from these statements. Understanding these statements will greatly aid in making sense of the financial terminology that can be encountered on a day-to-day basis.

3. Finally, and most importantly for our purposes, the 4 figure trick focuses on four figures all of which are contained within these financial statements, so it's essential we know how to locate these figures within these documents.

We're now going to look at each of these financial statements in turn. Pay particular attention to the logic in terms of what they're trying to tell us and, as already mentioned, the jargon. Don't worry too much about all the detail or how they're structured. As already mentioned, there are only four numbers we'll be interested in anyway. Let's start with the balance sheet. Here's a typical layout:

Maykitt & Sellitt Inc. balance sheet as at 31 December

	Latest year $m	Previous year $m
Non-current assets	63	61
Current assets	88	78
TOTAL ASSETS	151	139
Current liabilities	-62	-57
Non-current liabilities	-29	-28
NET ASSETS	**60**	**54**
Capital	14	14
Reserves	46	40
SHAREHOLDERS' FUNDS	**60**	**54**

The first point to note about a balance sheet is the title. A balance sheet is a valuation at a single point in time and, in the case of Maykitt & Sellitt, the valuation is as at 31 December in a given year. The second point is that it's common practice to provide previous year comparisons.

Now to the detail. Despite all the figures, this is in fact a remarkably straightforward document: it's nowhere near as bad as it may at first appear. Bear in mind, a balance sheet is simply a statement of wealth. Suppose you want to know what you're worth right now – where would you start? Logic says you should start off by adding up everything you own, and the jargon for things you own is assets. That's exactly what we can see happening in the example shown: the company starts off by adding up its assets.

In the corporate world it's common practice to divide assets into two types – non-current and current. Non-current assets are also sometimes referred to as fixed assets. Indeed, this latter title more accurately depicts what we're dealing with here. A non-current asset is something owned that is fixed in nature or, to be more precise, is an item that's owned where the intention is to keep it in its current form for more than one year. Examples of non-current assets in a company could include property, vehicles, computer equipment and office furniture. It must be emphasized that assets refers to items that are owned. If a company rents an office building, it doesn't own it, so it wouldn't be classed as an asset.

Moving on to current assets: these are things that are owned that will either be consumed or turned into something else within the next year. A good example of a current asset is inventory, where the intention will be to either sell it or utilize it within the next 12 months. Another commonly encountered current asset is debtors, where debtors refers to amounts owed to the business. The most common type of debtor is customers who have made purchases on credit, in which instance they are often referred to as accounts receivable. The third type of current asset commonly encountered is cash itself. Companies don't acquire cash to admire it, they acquire cash to spend it. Although there are other types of current asset, inventory, debtors and cash are the three types you're most likely to encounter in practice.

Adding together the non-current and the current assets tells you the total value of everything the company owns. Looking at the latest year for Maykitt & Sellitt, we can see the company has $63 million worth of non-current assets and $88 million worth of current assets, giving a total assets figure of $151 million. From an investors' point of view, the distinction between current and non-current assets is significant because it gives a sense of the company's liquidity (where liquidity means having ready access to cash). Cash is a key issue in every business, and lack of liquidity is a common cause of business failure.

Non-current assets, as we now know, refers to assets where the intention is to keep them in their current form for more than a year. By contrast, current assets refers to assets that already exist in the form of cash or will be translated into cash in the near future. Inventory is an asset that will be turned into cash within the next few months either through a direct sale or by incorporating it into something else that will be sold. Debtors refers to cash owed to the business that will be collected within the next 12 months. It follows that a company whose assets are primarily non-current could encounter significant financial difficulties if there is a downturn in sales, far more so than a company where most of its assets are current. Consider a car manufacturer, where huge sums of money are invested in production facilities. Such a business can be very exposed to the vagaries of the market. On the other hand, an online retailer may have very few non-current assets and therefore may find it easier to weather adverse trading conditions. This doesn't mean businesses shouldn't invest in non-current assets. Indeed, many businesses couldn't trade without non-current assets, but it's important management is aware of the inherent risks and have strategies in place to mitigate those risks. One of the worst situations any business can get itself into is needing cash and not being able to access it.

Returning to your personal example, imagine you've just written down everything you own. Maybe you own a house, a car, furniture, savings accounts, investments and so on. That's the enjoyable bit out of the way. Now you come onto the depressing part, because it's at this stage you need to detail everything you owe. Amounts owed are known as liabilities and, just as in the case of assets, companies typically divide these into two distinct categories – current and non-current.

Current liabilities are amounts owed that are payable within the next 12 months such as amounts owed to suppliers, payments owed to employees, taxes payable to the government and bank overdrafts. Non-current liabilities, as you've probably already worked out, are amounts owed that are payable after 12 months. These primarily tend to be forms of long-term borrowing. At a personal level, a mortgage would be a classic example of a non-current liability.

We're now in a position to work out what the company is worth. Returning to the example of Maykitt & Sellitt where the latest total asset figure is $151 million, if we deduct current liabilities worth $62 million and non-current liabilities worth $29 million, we can see that the company is valued at $60 million. The technical term for this figure is net assets. This tells us, in theory at least, if the company closes down tomorrow, sells off everything it owns and pays off everything it owes, the shareholders would walk away with $60 million. This is the value of their investment.

The last part of the balance sheet re-examines the net assets figure, but instead of looking at it in terms of assets and liabilities, it looks at the figure from a shareholder's point of view. When doing this it's common practice to divide shareholders' funds into two distinct elements – capital and reserves. In Chapter 2 we noted that there are only two ways shareholders can invest money in a company. One way is to hand over cash in exchange for shares. This is what we mean by capital. The only other way shareholders can invest money is, when a company declares a profit, the shareholders say, 'Keep it; reinvest it back into the business'. This is what we mean by reserves. Add together the capital and the reserves and you've got the total value of shareholders' funds. By the way – another title you may encounter on a balance sheet for shareholders' funds is equity.

The net assets figure and the shareholders' funds figure will always be the same, by definition. If the business has net assets worth $60 million, it follows the value of the shareholders' investment must be $60 million. It's impossible for these two figures to differ, because the reserves figure will always ensure they equate. Looking at the latest year's figures in the balance sheet for Maykitt & Sellitt, we can see that the value of the company's net assets is $60 million and we can also see the amount of capital originally invested in the company in exchange for shares was $14 million. It follows that there is a profit of $46 million currently locked inside the business (this being the difference between the original investment and what the business is worth now). That has to be the reserves figure.

As a small aside, it's often thought a balance sheet is so called because the net assets figure and the shareholders' funds figure will always balance. Even though that's true, that's not why it's called a balance sheet. The reason it's so called is because it's a list of balances. It tells us the balance on our non-current assets, the balance on our current assets and so on. That's why it's called a balance sheet; very few people know this!

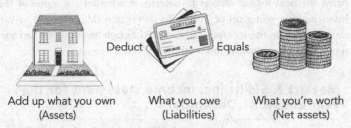

| Add up what you own | Deduct | What you owe | Equals | What you're worth |
| (Assets) | | (Liabilities) | | (Net assets) |

THE BALANCE SHEET MEASURES WEALTH

Before moving on from the balance sheet, there are a couple of points you ought to be aware of when looking at this financial statement for real. First of all, there tends to be a lot more detail provided than in the example shown. For example, non-current assets may be broken down into property, office equipment and so on. Notwithstanding this, the key components always remain unchanged, and for our purposes it's all we need to be aware of. Also, the format of balance sheets can alter from one company to another. What follows is an alternative format that may be encountered in practice. The key components remain unchanged: it's simply the order in which they appear that has altered.

Maykitt & Sellitt Inc. balance sheet as at 31 December

	Latest year $m	Previous year $m
Non-current assets	63	61
Current assets	88	78
TOTAL ASSETS	**151**	**139**
Current liabilities	62	57
Non-current liabilities	29	28
Shareholders' funds		
Capital	14	14
Reserves	46	40
TOTAL LIABILITIES AND EQUITY	**151**	**139**

Having established the value of the shareholders' investment in a company, the next logical step is to determine whether the value of that investment is going up or down. To determine this, we need to turn our attention to the income statement. Although terminology can vary, most income statements follow the same basic format.

Maykitt & Sellitt Inc. income statement for the year ended 31 December

	Latest year $m	Previous year $m
Revenue	150	133
Cost of sales	-59	-53
GROSS PROFIT	91	80
Operating expenses	-74	-68
OPERATING PROFIT	17	12
Interest payable	-2	-2
PROFIT BEFORE TAX	15	10
Tax	-3	-2
NET PROFIT	**12**	**8**

As is the case with the balance sheet, it's common practice to provide comparative figures for the previous year. Unlike the balance sheet, though, which provides a valuation of a business at a point in time, the income statement summarizes activity over a period of time – in this case, a year.

Before we study each of the components, we need to get a commonly held misconception out of the way. It's a widely held belief that an income statement is summarizing the revenues and costs during a period and, at first glance, that does indeed appear to be what's happening. I can't emphasize enough how important the next sentence is. An income statement doesn't summarize revenues and costs during a period!

The role of the income statement is to identify the profit made during a period; we noted in the previous chapter that profit measures changes in wealth – not changes in cash. As a result, the calculation of profit isn't quite as straightforward as you might at first think:

Profit = Revenue in a period
LESS The costs incurred to produce that revenue

This is definitely not the same thing as adding up revenue in a period and deducting the costs during that period.

Suppose you buy a car in January for $3,000 and then sell it for $4,000 in February. We will now apply the profit calculation to each month. In January there are no sales, so it follows there can't have been any costs to achieve that month's sales; therefore reported profit will be nil. What this is telling us is that your wealth during that month is unchanged, and we can see this is the case. You started off the month with $3,000 cash but ended up with $3,000 worth of car. We know the car is worth $3,000 because we watched you spend the money. The profit calculation is right – your wealth is unchanged. Now we'll apply the profit calculation to February. In that month you sell the car for $4,000, so, according to the profit calculation, we must now deduct whatever you spent to generate that sale, which is the $3,000 you spent buying the car back in January. This gives you a profit of $1,000 for the month, which again we can verify. From a wealth perspective, you started off the month with $3,000 worth of car but you end the month with $4,000 cash. The profit calculation is right again – you are indeed $1,000 better off at the end of the month than you were at the start.

Why is this important? According to the profit calculation, you make nil profit in January (there's no change in your wealth) but you make $1,000 profit in February (your wealth increases by $1,000). Compare this against what happens to cash. At the end of January you have $3,000 less cash than you had at the start of the month, while at the end of February you end up with $4,000 more cash than you had at start of that month. These figures are completely different from the profit figures for each month. This is a critical issue because what it tells us is that the calculation of profit makes no reference to when cash is received or when cash is paid out. The point to note here is that profit and cash flow are measuring very different things. The trouble is, businesses need cash to meet their financial commitments as they arise.

It follows there are two criteria that must be satisfied for any company to succeed financially:

- It must deliver *healthy profits* (create wealth) to keep the shareholders happy.

- It must deliver *healthy cash flow* to meet its financial commitments.

Deliver healthy profits   Deliver healthy cash flow

THERE ARE TWO CRITERIA FOR FINANCIAL SUCCESS

The good news is, in the short term at least, companies can survive without making profit. There are regular instances of companies reporting losses. However, a company can't survive without cash flow. If it can't pay its bills, it will cease trading pretty quickly.

The fact that making profit is not the same as generating cash flow should always be borne in mind whenever studying an income statement. Consequently, if a company is reporting healthy profits in its income statement, it doesn't necessarily follow the business is financially secure. Some time ago I was working with a major vehicle repair company. The bulk of their business involved repairing vehicles on behalf of insurance companies, since most of the repairs emanated from insurance claims. They decided to install a new accounts system, and, rather than go for a gradual transition from the old system, they decided to opt for the quick solution and to switch systems overnight. What resulted was chaos. For several months they had no idea who owed them money or how much. As a result, it took them almost 18 months to finally collect all the monies they were due. In the meantime they were reporting healthy profits (they were still raising lots of invoices); but the company came very close to collapse as there was no cash coming in to pay the bills.

Having established what an income statement is trying to tell us, we can now start to look at the content in a bit more depth. An income statement will always start off with the revenue figure (also sometimes called sales or turnover). This is the value of sales generated during the period, regardless of whether any cash has been received. Suppose a company raises an invoice on a client for services rendered. Even if the client hasn't paid the invoice yet, a sale has taken place, and that will be included in the company's revenue figure. From here on in, the income statement will confine attention exclusively to the costs that have been incurred to produce that period's revenue.

The first major cost category we encounter is usually called cost of sales. This refers to the direct costs of producing the sales achieved during the period. Suppose during a month a pen retailer buys 1,000 pens and during the same month sells 700. The income statement will only include the cost of the 700 pens sold, not the 1,000 bought. If you were a car manufacturer, it would be the manufacturing costs of the cars sold during the period that would appear in the income statement, not the cost of the cars coming off the production line. In companies that deal exclusively with products (as opposed to services), this expense is sometimes referred to as cost of goods sold, which very accurately describes exactly what this cost represents.

Deducting cost of sales from revenue brings us down to the first key profit figure – gross profit. This tells us how much profit has been made after only deducting the costs directly attributable to the products and services sold during the period. In other words, gross profit refers to the profit that has been made before deducting the day-to-day operating expenses of the business.

Next, we deduct all the operating expenses. These are the indirect expenses – what are sometimes referred to as overheads – and these would usually include functions such as information technology, human resources and finance.

Deducting operating expenses from gross profit brings us down to our next profit measure – operating profit. This can enjoy a wide variety of titles such as operating income, trading profit, profit before interest and tax (PBIT) and earnings before interest and tax (EBIT). This is the profit the company has made after paying for all its direct and indirect costs. In essence, this is the profit figure managers have generated through their judicious management of sales and costs. The remainder of this financial statement is dedicated to how this profit is to be distributed. Consequently, the operating profit line can be viewed as a breakpoint that divides the income statement into two discrete sections: everything above this line is about the revenue and costs of the business, while everything below this line is about how the resultant profit is distributed.

To fully comprehend the rest of the income statement, you need to appreciate how businesses are financed. If you were going to set up your own business, where would you get the money from? You have two basic options: you can either raise the money from investors or you can borrow it. But who will insist that they get their money back first? The answer is the people providing the loan finance, because, as far as they're concerned, this is a strict loan arrangement and they should not be exposed to unnecessary risk. It's the investors who are assuming the risk, and, as such, they come last in the queue. This explains how the remainder of the income statement is structured.

After operating profit, the first distribution is the interest payable on any loan finance that has been provided. This brings us down to the profit before tax line. Having allowed for the interest due to the providers of loan finance, you could be forgiven for thinking that whatever is left over must surely be attributable to the shareholders. Regrettably, this is rarely the case. In addition to shareholders and providers of loan finance, in most countries there's another party interested in getting a slice of the profit – the government. Most governments around the world impose a tax on corporate profits, and it's when we get down to the profit before tax line that they take their slice of any profits that have been made.

After having paid any tax due, at long last we arrive at the profit that has been made for shareholders – net profit. This is also sometimes called net income, profit after tax or profit available to shareholders. This is shareholders' money which they can do with as they please.

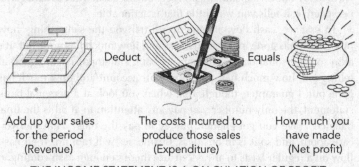

| Add up your sales for the period (Revenue) | Deduct | The costs incurred to produce those sales (Expenditure) | Equals | How much you have made (Net profit) |

THE INCOME STATEMENT IS A CALCULATION OF PROFIT

By the way – most income statements stop at net profit but, to complete our understanding of this particular report, it's worth considering what happens to this money. We've already noted that shareholders have two basic options available regarding what they can do with profit earned: they can either withdraw it in the form of a dividend or they can reinvest it back into the business. It's time to make sense of dividend strategy.

Suppose a company is doing really well and the future looks bright. Should it pay out a high or a low level of dividend? At first sight, the answer may appear to go against logic, because in this situation most companies would want to pay out a low dividend. Why? Suppose the company pays you a dividend. What are you going to do with the money? Put it in a savings account and earn a few percentage points in the form of interest? Alternatively, why not leave it in the business which could deliver a return on your funds of 10 per cent, maybe 20 per cent or even more. It's when companies are faced with limited growth opportunities they tend to favour paying out dividends. You can see this in practice. High-growth companies (such as those in the technology sector) tend to pay out very low dividends or in some instances no dividends at all. It tends to be the more mature businesses (such as those found in the utilities sector) that pay out the higher dividends. Indeed, many companies tend to do a bit of both: pay out dividends and reinvest.

There's just one more financial statement to go which is the cash flow statement. The good news is we're not going to explore this document. 'But why?' I hear you cry. First, because there are a variety of ways to lay out this document, and second, because, from a managerial perspective, it tells you very little that is actionable.

In essence, cash flow statements all tell you the same thing: how much cash has gone into the business and how much has gone out. It's akin to a personal bank statement. A bank statement is very good at telling you how much has gone into your account and how much has gone out. I guarantee, though, that when you look at a personal bank statement, the only number you pay any attention to at all is the final balance. Have you got enough money to pay the bills? That's all you care about, and so it is in business. Businesses will monitor their cash flow on a regular basis to always ensure there's enough cash coming in to meet their financial commitments, but that, in most instances, is as far as their interest goes.

The most important reason, though, for not needing to analyse cash flow statements, is there's another financial statement that tells us where all the cash is tied up anyway. If you think about it, the balance sheet tells us how much cash a business has tied up in property, equipment, vehicles, inventory and so forth. As a result, it's the balance sheet we use to manage the cash flow within a business, not the cash flow statement.

What we've just established is that, although there are three key financial statements, only two are needed to effectively manage a business:

1. The *balance sheet* is used to manage the cash within a business.

2. The *income statement* is used to manage the profit within a business.

Granted, there's been a lot to take in as we've progressed through this chapter – lots of jargon and financial concepts – but it's not been in vain. In the opening paragraph of this book I made a bold claim. I said that I'd show you how, in under one minute, you can ascertain whether a business is a success or not. You're about to find out how this is done.

To do this we need to return to the balance sheet. Normally, the first financial statement most people look at when examining an annual report is the income statement: they want to see if the company has made a profit or a loss. Bad move! The first document you should always look at is the balance sheet. Why? Because the balance sheet drives the company. All the sales budgets, all the cost budgets and so forth emanate from the balance sheet. A commonly held belief is that, when the directors sit down to set the budget for the year, they have some mystical insight into what the company is going to do over the ensuing months. In reality, they have no idea – nobody does. And guessing what the future holds is not where budgets should come from anyway.

As we've seen, a balance sheet is great at telling you what a company owns and what it owes; but it can also tell you something far more powerful. It can tell you how much profit a company ought to be making. Don't confuse this with how much profit a company *is* making – the income statement will tell you that.

We've already established the ultimate measure of financial success is return on equity and we've also established the minimum acceptable rate of return is 10 per cent. Combining these two pieces of information provides us with a powerful, yet simple to apply, diagnostic tool.

The balance sheet tells us the value of shareholders' funds within a company and, in the case of Maykitt & Sellitt, we noted that figure is currently $60 million. We also know that the minimum acceptable rate of return is 10 per cent, so it follows that this company needs to be making a net profit of at least $6 million. We can now turn our attention to the company's income statement and go straight to the net profit figure. If it's earning $6 million or more, we know the company is doing well. If it's earning less than $6 million, we know more work needs to be done. In the case of Maykitt & Sellitt, we can see from the income statement that during the last year the company delivered a $12 million profit. We can conclude from this that the company is doing pretty well – and we haven't even had to touch a calculator. The really good news is that this can all be done in well under a minute!

Take 10 per cent of shareholders' funds on the balance sheet

Is net profit on the income statement higher or lower than this figure?

HOW TO ASSESS COMPANY PERFORMANCE – FAST

What we've been introduced to so far is a quick intuitive method for assessing business performance, without the need for a calculator. In the case of Maykitt & Sellitt we've established it's achieving a return on equity that is well in excess of 10 per cent. What we haven't established, though, is the actual return on equity being achieved. To close off this chapter we're going to look at how to calculate an accurate figure, and to do this we need to revisit how return on equity is calculated:

$$\text{Return on equity} = \frac{\text{Net profit}}{\text{Average shareholders' funds}} \times 100\%$$

Identifying the net profit figure for the year is easy. We simply read it from the income statement which we know in the case of Maykitt & Sellitt is $12 million. Identifying average shareholders' funds isn't quite so straightforward. The problem with shareholders' funds as quoted on the balance sheet is that it's always the value at the end of the year, but what we need is the average value during the year. Time to return to some rudimentary mathematics. We can see that shareholders' funds at the end of the latest year is $60 million and that at the end of the previous year it was $54 million. Taking an average of these two figures tells us that the average value of shareholders' funds during the year was $57 million; this is the figure we need to perform the return on equity calculation:

$$\textbf{Return on equity} = \frac{\text{Net profit of \$12 million}}{\substack{\text{Average shareholders' funds} \\ \text{of \$57 million}}} \times 100\%$$

$$= 21\%$$

We now know Maykitt & Sellitt has achieved a return on equity of 21 per cent over the last year. The main preoccupation of managers, of course, should be the future. Is this level of profitability sustainable? Can it be improved? Where should management be focusing its attention going forward? As we shall discover, addressing questions like these is where the 4 figure trick will come into its own, but, before we can look at how to drive the business forward, we need to establish how the company achieved this rate of return in the first place. In other words, we need to understand how Maykitt & Sellitt actually makes profit. This forms the subject matter of the next chapter – understanding the profit-making process.

CHAPTER 4

The Profit-making Process

• • •

In the previous chapter we established some important financial principles. We know that in order to survive, a company must deliver on two things:

1. It must deliver *healthy profits* (create wealth) to keep the shareholders happy.

2. It must deliver *healthy cash flow* to meet its financial commitments.

We've also established that, although there are three key financial statements, only two are needed to effectively manage a business:

1. The *balance sheet* is used to manage the cash within a business.

2. The *income statement* is used to manage the profit within a business.

These conclusions are consistent with generally accepted financial wisdom. It's at this stage we start to deviate significantly from the conventional approach to financial management. The 4 figure trick argues that sound financial management is far more straightforward than is often made out. Indeed, in Chapter 2 we moved away from conventional wisdom by advocating that there's only one overriding measure of financial success – return on equity. This is in stark contrast to many exponents of financial management who would advocate that there are a range of measures that need to be looked at to determine whether or not a business is doing well. Why the disparity?

It all comes down to the question you're trying to answer. Most books on financial management ask the 'what' question. What's a balance sheet? What's an income statement? What measures of success are available? The answers to these questions create awareness, but awareness on its own is of no use when it comes to making decisions. To make sound decisions you need to ask the 'why' question. Asking, 'What is global warming?' can create awareness of an often discussed topic, but asking, 'Why is global warming an issue?' is what can provoke action. Many finance professionals focus on the 'what'. What happened to sales last week? What happened to costs last week? What is the current level of inventory? Managers should be far more concerned with the 'why'. Why are sales doing badly? Why are we overspending on costs? Why are inventory levels increasing? Understanding why things happen is the key to making sound decisions.

Back in Chapter 2, we determined return on equity is the ultimate measure of financial performance. This wasn't achieved by asking the question, 'What measures of financial performance are available?' – to which there are numerous answers. Instead, we asked the question 'Why do companies exist?' It was by asking this latter question that we were able to establish that the primary reason companies exist is to provide a return to shareholders. That led us to the single measure that is used to assess how effectively this is being done – return on equity.

It follows that, from a financial perspective, what managers need to understand in order to run a successful business is how to deliver a return on equity. Nothing more, nothing less. Let's revisit how it's calculated:

$$\textbf{Return on equity} = \frac{\text{Net profit}}{\text{Average shareholders' funds}} \times 100\%$$

This isn't just a measure. As mentioned previously, this is summarizing a process – a process which starts when shareholders invest cash in a business and finishes when the management team declares a profit. If you want to make sound business decisions, you don't need to understand all the intricacies of the financial world. All you need to understand is how to turn shareholders' funds into profit because, from a shareholders' perspective, that's your role.

It's a bit like a car. A car is a very complex piece of kit, and you do need quite a technical mind to understand how it all works. However, to drive a car you don't need to concern yourself with all these technicalities. All you need to understand are the basic controls and how to use them. The same is true in business. When you immerse yourself in the detail, there are indeed many intricacies underpinning the financial operations of a company. That's where the finance team comes into play: their role is to make sure the financial machine is working properly. As a business manager your objective is different: all you need to understand are the financial levers available to drive the business forward and how to operate them.

The 4 figure trick focuses attention on the levers available to enhance financial performance but, in order to do this, it demands a sound understanding of how companies literally translate shareholders' funds into profit; and it's developing this understanding that's the focus of this chapter. Don't underestimate what we're about to do here. Understanding how companies make profit is the key to making sound business decisions. Take time out to fully understand this chapter because everything else we cover builds on the principles we're going to examine here.

Like any process, profit-making can be broken down into stages, and in this instance there are three. The really good news is that these three stages are the same for every type of company regardless of whether it's a retailer, a car manufacturer or an oil exploration business. To understand what the three stages are we need to start at the beginning of the process with shareholders' funds. This is another classic example of how 'what' and 'why' can produce very different answers. If we asked the question, 'What do shareholders do?', a commonly held belief is that their primary role is to provide finance in order to enable the business to trade. However, if we ask the question, 'Why do companies need shareholders?', we get a very different answer. Indeed, the answer to this question suggests that companies need shareholders for a far more specific purpose, and, if you want to be a financially astute manager, it's essential that you understand what this purpose is.

One way to appreciate the role of shareholders is to examine a business that doesn't need any shareholders. Whenever I'm presenting the 4 figure trick I always try to come up with a product that captures the imagination. One product that often seems to achieve this and, consequently, is one that I use on many occasions is edible plates. Next time you have friends around for dinner, you don't give them a dessert – they can eat the plate instead. And the really good news is there's no washing up!

Suppose you've decided edible plates are the future and you're going to seize on this market opportunity by setting up your own edible plate business. Being the shrewd businessperson that you are, you insist on receiving payment with each order, and things go well during your first month of trading – you manage to secure orders totalling $60,000. You then contact a supplier and arrange for edible plates to be shipped directly to your customers at a cost of $50,000, leaving you with a profit of $10,000. This is all that happens during the first month.

Now comes the critical question. How much money did you have to invest to start the business off? The answer is nil because, by insisting customers pay cash with their orders, you don't need to raise any funds from investors: your customers are financing the entire operation. This proves it's possible to start up a business without the need for any investors. Regrettably, this is an extremely rare occurrence!

Let's revisit this business with a slight timing adjustment. Instead of approaching your customers first, you decide to approach the supplier first and, as previously, you pay $50,000 for the plates. You then sell these plates to your customers for $60,000, leaving once again a profit of $10,000. Now, how much money did you have to invest to start the business off? In this latter scenario you needed to raise $50,000 at the outset. You may have provided these funds yourself or you may have chosen to raise at least some of the funds from other investors. This is in stark contrast to the original scenario where no initial investment was required at all. This begs a question: what's changed?

The reason you now need funds from investors is to enable you to purchase the plates. The point to note is that, until they're sold, the business will own these plates. In other words, for a while at least, these plates will be assets. We've just identified the role of shareholders – companies need shareholders to finance assets.

This is the first stage of the profit-making process. If you're about to start up your own business, you can forget about sales and you can forget about costs. The opening move is to raise funds to finance assets. By the way – this can make or break you right from the word go. Suppose you want to set up your own business and have decided you want luxurious offices, an expensive car, cutting-edge computer equipment and top-quality office furniture: in other words, you want lots of assets. It follows that you'll need to raise a lot of funds to finance these assets. The problem is, raising lots of funds demands a high level of profit in order to provide a decent rate of return on those funds, which in turn demands a high level of sales. You've just managed to put enormous pressure on your sales figure and you haven't even started trading yet. By contrast, if you start up your business with minimal assets, you won't need to raise a lot of funds, which means you only need a modest level of profit to provide a decent rate of return on those funds. This takes the pressure right off your sales figure.

If you work in an office and you have a desk and a desktop computer, those are assets and they've been funded by shareholders. The problem is, shareholders want a return on that investment, and the only way this can be done is through sales. The very fact you have a desk and a desktop computer is putting pressure on the sales target: that's how direct the link is between assets and sales. The more assets you have the more sales you need to generate a decent level of profit. This explains, for example, why the retail sector in many countries has witnessed a seismic shift from in-store sales to online sales. Acquiring a store in a prime location, fitting it out and filling it with inventory involves a lot of assets; having lots of assets demands lots of funding; and lots of funding demands lots of profit; and lots of profit demands lots of sales. By contrast, you can set up an online retail business in a shed in the middle of a field. Indeed, I'm aware of some online retail businesses that have literally done this! The big advantage of doing this is that it involves far fewer assets, thereby enabling online retailers to provide a decent rate of return on funds raised with far fewer sales.

The fact that shareholders' funds are needed to finance assets raises a question. Where does the money come from to pay day-to-day expenses such as salaries, office supplies and rent? These are all paid for out of sales. Consequently, there are two distinct cash flows into any business:

1. Shareholders provide cash to finance assets.

2. Sales provide cash to pay the day-to-day expenses.

There's another way companies can finance assets, though: they can borrow – but why would any company want to borrow money if it can raise it from shareholders? If a business raises money from shareholders and fails to make a profit, there's no obligation to pay dividends, but if it borrows money it has to pay interest regardless of whether or not a profit is made. This would seem to suggest that companies should always raise funds from shareholders wherever possible and resist the temptation to borrow. However, there's a very strong commercial argument for borrowing money, and it's one that's not at all obvious.

On a personal level, you may well dream of the day you finally pay off all those debts – the mortgage, the car loan and the credit cards. This doesn't apply in the corporate world. Believe it or not, many businesses love debt; and the reason they love it is because it can help improve return on equity. Strange as it may sound, in the business world, debt can be your best friend. Let's see how this works.

We will now return to your edible plate business where you needed to invest $50,000 to finance plates which you subsequently sold for $60,000, leaving a profit of $10,000. In this instance your return on equity was 20 per cent ($10,000 profit as a percentage of your $50,000 investment). Suppose that, in addition to your $50,000 investment, you decide to take out a bank loan for an additional $50,000. This will enable you to buy $100,000 worth of plates which you should be able to sell potentially for $120,000. The problem with borrowing money, of course, is that you have to pay interest. If you're being charged 10 per cent on the loan, out of the $20,000 you're now making buying and selling the plates, you'll have to pay the bank $5,000 interest (10 per cent of the $50,000 loan). This will reduce your profit to $15,000, but now comes the exquisite twist. How much of your money has been invested in this venture? The answer is still $50,000. That means that you've just made $15,000 profit on your $50,000 investment, giving you a 30 per cent return on equity. You've just increased your rate of return from 20 to 30 per cent; and all you've done is borrow money.

It's often argued that another problem with borrowing money, in addition to having to pay interest, is that you have to pay the loan back. Ironically, for many companies paying off a loan is not perceived as a problem, and that's because they've no intention of ever paying it off. In the corporate world, borrowings are often regarded as a permanent facility, and there's logic behind this. We've just established that by borrowing money the return to shareholders can be increased. This suggests that, if a loan is paid off, the return to shareholders could drop, and shareholders definitely wouldn't be happy about that. Also, the lenders wouldn't be happy either because they only earn interest while the money is out on loan. So, by paying off a loan, a company could end up upsetting both its shareholders and its lenders. Why upset people? Don't pay off the loan, and then everyone's happy!

Based on the discussion so far it might appear that, if a company wants to be successful, all it has to do is borrow vast quantities of money. Real life says the situation isn't quite that straightforward: things can go wrong. What happens if the company fails to make its planned sales figure? Everything rotates around this number.

Suppose that, in the latest version of your edible plate business, your sales come in at $115,000 instead of $120,000. In this instance you'll be making $15,000 buying and selling plates ($115,000 sales less $100,000 spent on the plates) but, after paying $5,000 interest to the bank, your profit would drop back down to the original level of $10,000. It follows that, if sales come in at more than $5,000 below the planned figure of $120,000 (which is only just over a four per cent drop), you'll end up achieving a return on equity that's lower than it would have been if you'd only generated $60,000 worth of sales with no borrowing at all. That's the risk.

This is a valuable lesson. Borrowing funds can benefit companies that are able to deliver robust sales each year, but it can cause serious problems for businesses whose sales performance is more erratic. One counter-argument to this piece of logic is that not all borrowed funds are subject to interest charges. For instance, a company might obtain 30 days' credit from its suppliers. No interest is typically applicable in this situation, but even here there's still risk involved. The company could become reliant on the continuing existence of that credit facility so that, if ever the facility should be withdrawn, it might struggle, and that's most likely to occur when sales in a business are falling. So the basic logic holds true. Borrowing money can improve return on equity, but it also exposes the company to two risks: failure to meet interest commitments and/or increased reliance on credit facilities to continue trading.

It follows, when assessing how effectively a company is managing the profit-making process, the first issue that needs to be addressed is how it raises its funds. Fortunately, there's a measure that can assist in this instance called gearing (also known as leverage). This looks at the proportion of funds raised by a business that have been borrowed. Although there are a number of devious ways to calculate gearing that are used by accountants, these are of no relevance to us. From a managerial perspective, all we want to know is what proportion of funds raised are borrowed and this can be worked out quite simply as follows:

$$\text{Gearing} = \frac{\text{Average liabilities}}{\text{Average assets}} \times 100\%$$

This calculation looks at liabilities (total amounts owed) as a percentage of the total funds invested in assets. You'll note that we're looking at average values here. This is because the value of assets and liabilities can change, so, if we want to assess performance over a period of time, logically we'll be interested in the average values over that period.

Let's look at the gearing in the latest scenario of your edible plate business where you acquire $100,000 worth of assets (plates) of which $50,000 worth is financed by shareholders and $50,000 worth is financed by borrowed funds.

$$\text{Gearing} = \frac{\text{Average liabilities of } \$50,000}{\text{Average assets of } \$100,000} \times 100\%$$

$$= 50\%$$

This tells us that, out of all the funds raised to finance assets, 50 per cent of them were borrowed.

When gearing is over 50 per cent (the majority of funds raised are borrowed), a company is said to be high geared. When gearing is less than 50 per cent (the majority of funds raised are from shareholders), it's said to be low geared. When the split is 50/50, it's said to be gearing neutral.

Low-geared companies don't tend to raise any alarm bells as their funding is indicative of low interest commitments and/or low reliance on third-party credit. By contrast, high-geared companies will always warrant further investigation. This is a situation where you need to study the company's sales performance. Provided the company is delivering robust sales each year, high gearing may well not be an issue. However, if sales are erratic, there could be problems ahead: the company may be unable to meet its interest commitments and/or credit facilities may be withdrawn.

So the first stage of the profit-making process says companies need to raise funds to finance assets, whether this be from shareholders or in the form of borrowings.

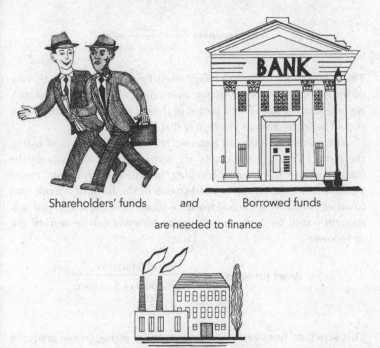

Shareholders' funds   *and*   Borrowed funds

are needed to finance

Assets

THE FIRST STAGE OF THE PROFIT-MAKING PROCESS

This brings us on to the second stage of the profit-making process. Having established that funds are needed to finance assets, it's time to ask another 'why' question. Why do companies need assets? The function of assets, whether directly or indirectly, is to generate sales. Whether money is being invested in inventory, equipment, vehicles, buildings or computer systems, the objective is always the same – to help generate sales. If you were setting up your own business, there's no way you would invest in any assets unless you were convinced that, somehow or other, those assets would help generate sales.

Not surprisingly, there's a measure that looks at how effectively a company is utilizing its assets to generate sales. It's called asset turnover and is worked out by dividing sales by average assets:

$$\text{Asset turnover} = \frac{\text{Sales}}{\text{Average assets}}$$

The argument for using an average assets figure is the same as that cited for gearing – assets can change over time. Because, in this instance, we're looking at sales over a period of time, it follows that our interest should be in the average assets over that same period.

The more sales you can generate from any given level of assets, the more effectively the assets are being utilized. Let's revisit the latest scenario for your edible plate business wherein you raised $50,000 from shareholders and $50,000 in the form of a bank loan in order to finance $100,000 worth of plates (assets), which you subsequently sold for $120,000. The asset turnover can be worked out as follows:

$$\text{Asset turnover} = \frac{\text{Sales of } \$120,000}{\text{Average assets of } \$100,000}$$

$$= 1.2$$

This says that, from every $1 you invested in assets, you've produced $1.20 worth of sales. The higher the number, the more effectively you're managing your assets and the higher your return on equity should be.

Don't underestimate the importance of asset turnover. Once funds have been raised to finance assets, the only source of cash subsequently available to a business is sales. We've already established that you need sales to pay day-to-day expenses, so it follows that there must be a link between asset turnover and cost management. If a company has a low asset turnover, the cash generation from its assets is low, which means it needs to keep a very tight rein on costs. By contrast, if a company has a high asset turnover, it's generating far more cash from its assets, allowing it to spend more on staffing, marketing and so on. Without adequate asset turnover, it's impossible to run a profitable business. This is the second stage of the profit-making process – using assets to generate sales.

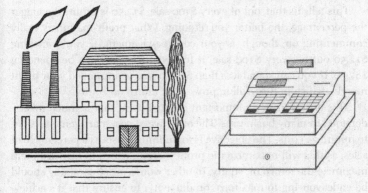

Assets   are needed to generate   Sales

THE SECOND STAGE OF THE PROFIT-MAKING PROCESS

Having established that the second stage of the profit-making process is all about turning assets into sales, it's time to ask yet another 'why' question. Why do companies want sales? The answer is to make profit. If a company reports that sales this year are 50 per cent up on last year, this may sound impressive; however, if profit is unaltered, the business is working harder but to no effect.

To assess how effectively the third stage of the process is being managed, there's yet another measure that comes to the rescue. Profit margin looks at net profit as a percentage of sales:

$$\textbf{Profit margin} = \frac{\text{Net profit}}{\text{Sales}} \times 100\%$$

Let's once again turn our attention to the latest scenario of your edible plate business where you bought plates for $100,000, subsequently sold them for $120,000, paid $5,000 in interest to the bank, leaving you with a profit of $15,000.

$$\textbf{Profit margin} = \frac{\text{Net profit of } \$15,000}{\text{Sales of } \$120,000} \times 100\%$$

$$= 12.5\%$$

This tells us that, out of every $100 sale, $12.50 is profit; the bigger the percentage, the better you're doing. What profit margin is really commenting on, though, is your cost management. If you're making $12.50 out of every $100 sale, it follows that you must be spending $87.50. If you can spend less than $87.50, you've improved your profit margin, which in turn will improve your return on equity.

This brings us to an important point: a point that is much misunderstood in many businesses. The objective of cost management is not to minimize costs. The objective is to minimize costs as a percentage of sales, as this will maximize the profit margin, which in turn will help maximize the return on equity. In other words, every company should be endeavouring to maximize productivity: to ensure that it's achieving the highest possible level of sales on every dollar spent. This is the third, and indeed final, stage of the profit-making process: turning sales into profit.

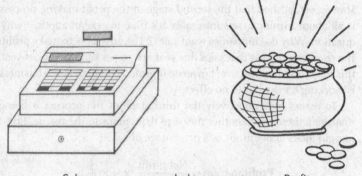

Sales   are needed to generate   Profit

THE THIRD STAGE OF THE PROFIT-MAKING PROCESS

Suppose a company enjoys an annual turnover of $100 million and spends $10 million on payroll, so that its payroll is running at 10 per cent of sales. If it can reduce this percentage, the profit margin will improve. It doesn't follow, though, that, in order to achieve this, the company needs to get rid of staff. One way to reduce the percentage is to make sure that, as sales increase, the payroll bill grows at a slower rate. In this situation, although expenditure on payroll might be increasing, as a percentage of sales the cost will have reduced, and that's what counts. Indeed, sometimes getting rid of staff might be the worst thing to do if it results in falling sales.

During our foray so far into the world of financial management, we've established some important principles:

- The ultimate measure of financial performance is return on equity.
- Delivering a healthy return on equity is a process that comprises three stages.
- In order to deliver a healthy return on equity, a business needs to generate healthy profit and healthy cash flow.

We're now in a position to see how these various concepts interrelate, and understanding this is a prerequisite to managing a financially successful business. The following diagram shows how the three stages of the profit-making process interrelate and also highlights which stages impact upon the cash flow of a company and which impact upon its profitability.

As can be seen, the first stage of the profit-making process involves raising funds to finance assets. How this has been achieved can be assessed using gearing, which states the proportion of funds raised that are borrowed. The second stage involves using these assets to generate sales. This can be assessed using asset turnover, which states the level of sales being generated from each dollar invested in assets. Finally, the third stage involves translating sales into profit. This can be assessed using profit margin, which states the proportion of each sale that is left over as profit, after paying all expenses.

The first two stages of the profit-making process are all about cash management. The first stage is all about raising cash to finance assets, while the second stage is all about translating assets back into cash in the form of sales. It's only the final stage that is true profit management, which involves ensuring that, when sales are generated, there's still a profit left over at the end of the day.

THE 4 FIGURE TRICK

Shareholders' funds *and* Borrowed funds

are needed to finance

This is
GEARING

Assets

which are needed to generate

This is
ASSET TURNOVER

These two stages affect a company's **CASH FLOW**

Sales

which are needed to generate

This is
PROFIT MARGIN

This stage affects a company's **PROFIT**

Profit

THE COMPLETE PROFIT-MAKING PROCESS

Every company, regardless of the industry within which it trades or its geographic location, goes through these three stages. The easiest way to fully grasp how these three stages interrelate is to imagine you're going to open a store. The first stage is deciding how you're going to finance it. If you're confident when you open the doors that customers are going to flood in, you should consider borrowing money and enjoy the high rate of return. However, if you're not sure how sales are going to perform, you should endeavour to keep your financial risk to a minimum and concentrate on raising the money from investors. That's the gearing stage. Having acquired the assets – the store, the fixtures, the inventory and so on – you can move on to the second stage. How good are you at using these assets to attract customers through the door and physically put money in the till? In other words, how good are you at using these assets to generate sales? That's the asset turnover stage. Finally, the third stage says: now you've got money in the till, but you've got bills to pay. How good are you at managing costs to ensure there's still a profit left over at the end of the day? That's the profit margin stage.

Looking at these three stages explains why so many businesses struggle. Regrettably, it's a common misconception that there are only two ways to improve business performance – either increase sales or cut costs. This explains why, in my experience, by far the main preoccupation for many managers I've worked with has been profit margin. Nearly all their attention has been directed towards sales and costs with no real awareness, or indeed interest, of assets or funding. By focusing almost exclusively on profit margin, they're looking at only one-third of the machine. All you need is one of the other stages of the profit-making process to go awry and it could herald the end of trading. The key to managing a successful business is managing the entire profit-making process – not just one section of it.

If everything we've covered in this chapter makes sense to you, we're now at long last poised to examine the 4 figure trick.

CHAPTER 5

It's All About 4 Figures

• • •

In the opening paragraph of this book, I made two promises. In Chapter 3 I fulfilled the first promise: I showed you how, in under one minute, you can ascertain whether a business is a success or not. Now we're going to address the second promise. I'm about to show you how, in less than five minutes, you can identify the core strengths and weaknesses within any business.

Let's revisit your edible plate business which was introduced in the previous chapter:

- You raised $50,000 from investors and a further $50,000 as a loan from a bank to finance the purchase of $100,000 worth of edible plates.
- You sold all the plates for $120,000.
- You paid $5,000 in interest to the bank.
- This left you with $15,000 profit.

On the basis of these figures we noted the return on equity was 30 per cent ($15,000 profit as a percentage of the $50,000 raised from investors). We then went on to calculate three further measures:

$$\text{Gearing} = \frac{\text{Average liabilities of } \$50,000}{\text{Average assets of } \$100,000} \times 100\%$$
$$= 50\%$$

$$\text{Asset turnover} = \frac{\text{Sales of \$120,000}}{\text{Average assets of \$100,000}}$$

$$= 1.2$$

$$\text{Profit margin} = \frac{\text{Net profit of \$15,000}}{\text{Sales of \$120,000}} \times 100\%$$

$$= 12.5\%$$

We know that improving any of these measures could potentially improve return on equity. However, up until now we've viewed these measures as three discrete calculations, where in reality, they're all inter-related. What we're now going to do is pull all of these results together into an analytical tool I created many years ago, which I call a *return on equity flowchart*. This will literally show us how you managed to turn $50,000 of investors' cash into $15,000 profit: in other words, it will show us how you managed to deliver a return on equity of 30 per cent.

GEARING is	50%
So for every $100 of funds raised …	↓
Shareholders provide	$50
Other sources provide	$50
Which is used to finance …	↓
Assets worth	$100
ASSET TURNOVER is	1.2
So every $100 worth of assets generates …	↓
Sales of	$120
PROFIT MARGIN is	12.5%
So sales of $120 generate …	↓
Profit of	$15
Which produces …	↓
RETURN ON EQUITY of	30%

A RETURN ON EQUITY FLOWCHART

When it comes to making sense of this analytical tool, the first point to note is that companies can vary in size, but we will inevitably want to be able to compare them. To facilitate this, a return on equity flowchart focuses attention on what happens to each $100 tranche of funds a company raises. This enables us to readily compare a company that is raising billions of dollars with a company that is raising just a few million. Having addressed this minor technicality, we can now turn our attention to the flowchart itself which can be broken down into three sections, mirroring the three stages of the profit-making process – gearing, asset turnover and profit margin.

As we know, the first stage of the profit-making process involves raising funds to finance assets, and how this is achieved can be measured in terms of gearing. In the case of your edible plate business, we established that the gearing was 50 per cent, which tells us that, out of every $100 raised, $50 was borrowed, implying the remaining $50 must have come from shareholders. This explains how you financed each $100 worth of assets (edible plates).

The flowchart now progresses to the second stage of the profit-making process which involves using assets to generate sales. Your edible plate business has an asset turnover of 1.2, which tells us that, from every $1 invested in assets, sales of $1.20 were generated. It follows that, from every $100 worth of assets in your business, sales of $120 were being generated.

The final section of the flowchart focuses on the third stage of the profit-making process – turning sales into profit. We noted that the profit margin in your edible plate business was found to be 12.5 per cent. In this flowchart we're looking at sales of $120, so 12.5 per cent of this figure must be profit, which works out at $15.

Looking towards the bottom of the flowchart, we can see that your edible plate business has made $15 profit on every $100 raised; and looking towards the top of the flowchart, we can also see that shareholders have needed to invest only $50 to achieve this level of profit. This explains how your edible plate business managed to produce a return on equity of 30 per cent. What we've identified here is a powerful analytical tool which can literally show us, step-by-step, how any company takes cash from its shareholders and turns it into profit.

A return on equity flowchart emphasizes the fact that the profit-making process is a combination of three elements – gearing, asset turnover and profit margin. What may not be so immediately apparent is that the calculation of all these measures requires just four figures:

1. Sales
2. Net profit
3. Average assets
4. Average shareholders' funds.

Welcome to the 4 figure trick! The 4 figure trick says every business is defined by these four figures, and it's how these four figures interrelate that will define whether a business turns out to be a success or a failure.

Sales

Net profit

Average assets

Average shareholders' funds

THE 4 FIGURE TRICK SAYS THAT EVERY BUSINESS IS DEFINED BY JUST FOUR FIGURES

The whole premise of the 4 figure trick is that, using just four numbers, we can gain significant insight into the financial machinations of any business and readily identify those areas that demand management attention. This is achieved through the creation of a return on equity flowchart.

By creating a return on equity flowchart for your edible plate business, we have in fact already worked through an application of the 4 figure trick, even if we didn't realize it. What we're going to do now is see how this analysis can be readily applied to the trading results of any company. We are about to work our way, step-by-step, from the extraction of the four figures through to the production of the return on equity flowchart. Like the profit-making process, this will involve three stages.

Before going any further, there is a little bit of bad news, I'm afraid: the 4 figure trick does involve performing a few calculations. If you want to really get inside the financial machinations of a company, there are inevitably going to be times when you need to reach for a calculator. The good news is that they can all be done in a matter of minutes, and that, most importantly, they'll enable you to glean far more understanding and insight into a company than many people can achieve spending several hours poring over a set of accounts. The effort will be worth it!

It's worth remembering that there are two different sets of accounts that managers will encounter in practice. First of all, there are the annual accounts, also known as the statutory accounts, the primary function of which is to inform shareholders of what the company has done with their money. During the year, additional interim accounts are also produced, known as management accounts, which are exclusively for internal use. For expositional purposes, we're going to confine our attention to the annual accounts. However, if you understand how to apply the 4 figure trick to a set of annual accounts, you'll have no problem applying it to a periodic set of management accounts, as the principles are identical.

In Chapter 3 we were introduced to the annual accounts of Maykitt & Sellitt, and we're going to use this company as a working example of how to apply the 4 figure trick to any business. Let's start by revisiting its income statement.

Maykitt & Sellitt Inc. income statement for the year ended 31 December

	Latest year $m	Previous year $m
Revenue	150	133
Cost of sales	-59	-53
GROSS PROFIT	91	80
Operating expenses	-74	-68
OPERATING PROFIT	17	12
Interest payable	-2	-2
PROFIT BEFORE TAX	15	10
Tax	-3	-2
NET PROFIT	**12**	**8**

According to the 4 figure trick we need to extract just two figures from this financial statement: sales and net profit. Sales is easy. This will appear at the top of the statement and, although it can enjoy a variety of titles, such as revenue and turnover, it's not difficult to spot. In this instance, we can see the latest annual sales figure for Maykitt & Sellitt is $150 million – so that's one figure done already.

The other figure we need is net profit (or profit after tax). This is usually the last figure that appears at the bottom of the statement. In this instance, we can see the net profit figure is $12 million. That's all we need from the income statement.

It's time to turn our attention to the balance sheet. The 4 figure trick says that there are two further figures we need to extract from this statement: average assets and average shareholders' funds. But we've hit a problem because, unlike an income statement that tells you what's happening over a period of time, a balance sheet is a snapshot at a point in time. If we're looking at sales and net profit generated over a year, logic says we should be looking at average assets and average shareholders' funds over the same period.

Maykitt and Sellitt Inc. balance sheet as at 31 December

	Latest year $m	Previous year $m
Non-current assets	63	61
Current assets	88	78
TOTAL ASSETS	151	139
Current liabilities	-62	-57
Non-current liabilities	-29	-28
NET ASSETS	**60**	**54**
Capital	14	14
Reserves	46	40
SHAREHOLDERS' FUNDS	**60**	**54**

Average assets and average shareholders' funds need to be worked out.

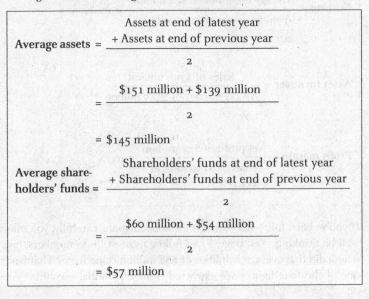

$$\text{Average assets} = \frac{\text{Assets at end of latest year} + \text{Assets at end of previous year}}{2}$$

$$= \frac{\$151 \text{ million} + \$139 \text{ million}}{2}$$

$$= \$145 \text{ million}$$

$$\text{Average shareholders' funds} = \frac{\text{Shareholders' funds at end of latest year} + \text{Shareholders' funds at end of previous year}}{2}$$

$$= \frac{\$60 \text{ million} + \$54 \text{ million}}{2}$$

$$= \$57 \text{ million}$$

I appreciate that this was a little bit fiddly, but now we have everything we need from the balance sheet. We can now put the annual accounts to one side – we don't need them anymore.

This is the first stage of the 4 figure trick. You need to extract just four figures from the annual report – sales, net profit, average assets and average shareholders' funds. Here are the four figures we've just extracted from the annual accounts of Maykitt & Sellitt:

Sales	$150 million
Net profit	$12 million
Average assets	$145 million
Average shareholders' funds	$57 million

The second stage of the 4 figure trick involves combining these four figures to create the three key measures we know impact upon financial performance: gearing, asset turnover and profit margin. In the case of Maykitt & Sellitt, they work out as follows:

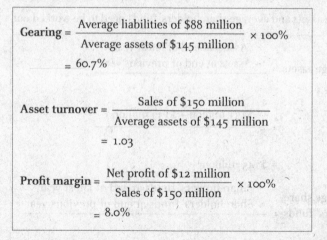

$$\text{Gearing} = \frac{\text{Average liabilities of \$88 million}}{\text{Average assets of \$145 million}} \times 100\%$$
$$= 60.7\%$$

$$\text{Asset turnover} = \frac{\text{Sales of \$150 million}}{\text{Average assets of \$145 million}}$$
$$= 1.03$$

$$\text{Profit margin} = \frac{\text{Net profit of \$12 million}}{\text{Sales of \$150 million}} \times 100\%$$
$$= 8.0\%$$

If you've been following through these calculations carefully, you may well be thinking, 'Yes, Dave, I can follow most of those numbers, but where did that average liabilities of $88 million come from? That isn't one of the four figures we extracted from the annual accounts.' We know that average assets during the year was $145 million and we know that average shareholders' funds – used to help finance those assets – was $57 million. It follows that the remaining $88 million must have been borrowed in some shape or form, so that has to be the average liabilities figure. To put it another way, average liabilities is simply the difference between average assets and average shareholders' funds.

This raises a question. When we were extracting figures from the balance sheet, why didn't we extract average liabilities instead of average shareholders' funds? There are two reasons we focus on shareholders' funds. First, whenever management looks at a set of accounts, the first issue it will always want to address is how the company is doing overall. This involves calculating the return on equity, and for this you need two figures: net profit and average shareholders' funds. Second, and this is a more practical point, when studying a balance sheet it's common to see a figure for total assets and also a figure for total shareholders' funds. It's far less common to see a figure for total liabilities being quoted. As a result, establishing an average total liabilities figure directly from a balance sheet can be a real pain, often involving adding several separate liability figures together.

This brings us onto the third and final stage of the 4 figure trick – the production of the return on equity flowchart. We know that the first stage of the profit-making process is gearing – raising funds to finance assets. In the case of Maykitt & Sellitt we have worked out gearing is 60.7 per cent, which tells us that, out of every $100 raised, $60.70 was borrowed. The remaining $39.30 must therefore be coming from shareholders. As we know, the reason these funds need to be raised is to finance assets. This is all we need to complete the first part of the flowchart:

GEARING is	60.7%
So for every $100 of funds raised …	↓
Shareholders provide	$39.30
Other sources provide	$60.70
Which is used to finance …	↓
Assets worth	$100

The second stage of the profit-making process is all about asset turnover – using assets to generate sales. The asset turnover for Maykitt & Sellitt is 1.03 which tells us that, from every $1 invested in assets during the year, sales of $1.03 were generated. Bear in mind that this flowchart is interested in what happens to each $100 raised, so, if we're generating $1.03 from every $1 invested in assets, it follows that from every $100 invested in assets we were generating sales of $103. We can now complete the next part of the flowchart:

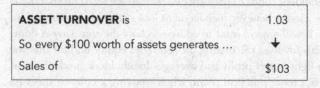

ASSET TURNOVER is	1.03
So every $100 worth of assets generates ...	↓
Sales of	$103

This leads us onto the final part of the profit-making process which is all about profit margin – turning sales into profit. Maykitt & Sellitt enjoyed a profit margin of 8 per cent, which means 8 per cent of sales is profit. In this instance, we're looking at a sales figure of $103, and 8 per cent of that figure gives us a profit of $8.24. We've already established that out of every $100 raised the shareholders have provided $39.30, so, if Maykitt & Sellitt are producing $8.24 profit on every $39.30 invested by shareholders, it follows that the company must be producing a return on equity of 21 per cent. This is all we need to know to complete the final section of the flowchart:

PROFIT MARGIN is	8.0%
So sales of $103 generate ...	↓
Profit of	$8.24
Which produces ...	↓
RETURN ON EQUITY of	21.0%

We can now combine all this information to create a complete return on equity flowchart showing how Maykitt & Sellitt managed to generate a return on equity of 21 per cent.

GEARING is	60.7%
So for every $100 of funds raised ...	↓
Shareholders provide	$39.30
Other sources provide	$60.70
Which is used to finance ...	↓
Assets worth	$100
ASSET TURNOVER is	1.03
So every $100 worth of assets generates ...	↓
Sales of	$103
PROFIT MARGIN is	8.0%
So sales of $103 generate ...	↓
Profit of	$8.24
Which produces ...	↓
RETURN ON EQUITY of	21.0%

The real power of the return on equity flowchart emerges when the latest year's performance is compared against the previous year. This will clearly highlight which areas are strengthening within the business and/or which are weakening. Also comparing against similar companies can prove to be an enlightening exercise. What is most pertinent is that we can glean all this information in less than five minutes.

Probably the most important conclusion we can draw from constructing a return on equity flowchart is that it highlights how there are only three ways any company can improve the return on shareholders' funds:

1. It can increase *gearing* (although this can also increase financial risk).

2. It can increase *asset turnover*.

3. It can increase *profit margin*.

Every manager in every business, regardless of their role, will be impacting on at least one of these measures. They can impact upon the level of borrowed funds by negotiating credit terms with suppliers. They can impact upon asset turnover simply by ordering new office furniture. They will definitely be impacting upon costs by the very fact they're being paid a salary. It follows that there are three questions any financially astute manager should be asking on a regular basis:

1. Is the business being appropriately funded?
2. Are assets being managed effectively?
3. Are costs being managed effectively?

To close off this chapter, let's summarize how to apply the 4 figure trick to any company:

Stage 1	Extract four figures from the annual accounts:
	• Sales
	• Net profit
	• Average assets
	• Average shareholders' funds.
	The first two figures are sourced from the income statement, while the last two figures are sourced from the balance sheet. You can now put the accounts to one side – you don't need them anymore.
Stage 2	Using these four figures, calculate the three key measures that impact upon financial performance:
	• Gearing
	• Asset turnover
	• Profit margin.
Stage 3	Combine gearing, asset turnover and profit margin to form a powerful analytical tool:
	• Return on equity flowchart.
	Comparing performance against previous years and other companies can readily highlight those areas where management attention may be required.

And don't forget, once the logic is firmly in place, all of this analysis can be achieved in less than five minutes.

CHAPTER 6

The Formula For Financial Success

● ● ●

The previous two chapters have been dedicated to understanding how companies make profit and how to assess past trading performance. To facilitate this we were introduced to a powerful analytical tool – the return on equity flowchart – which provides a fast and effective way of climbing inside a company and readily identifying its strengths and weaknesses. This information can prove invaluable when it comes to determining where management action is required. However, the 4 figure trick doesn't just enable us to diagnose how a business is performing and help us direct management attention: it can also prove to be a powerful aid when it comes to planning for the future.

A key element of making a sound business decision is having the discipline to assess its potential impact before the decision is ever made, and, by focusing attention on just four figures, the 4 figure trick greatly simplifies how this can be done.

At the heart of the 4 figure trick is a formula:

$$\text{Return on equity} = \frac{\text{Asset turnover} \times \text{Profit margin}}{(100 - \text{Gearing})} \times 100\%$$

If you're not particularly mathematically inclined, this may look a bit daunting, but don't be put off: once you understand the logic, it is in fact remarkably straightforward. All it's doing is summarizing the various relationships that exist within a return on equity flowchart. If you understand a return on equity flowchart, you're only one small step away from making sense of this formula.

In the previous chapter we constructed a return on equity flowchart for Maykitt & Sellitt, and when we were doing this we calculated three performance measures relating to the latest trading year:

Gearing   = 60.7%

Asset turnover   = 1.03

Profit margin   = 8.0%

Let's insert these numbers into our formula:

$$\textbf{Return on equity} = \frac{\text{Asset turnover of } 1.03 \times \text{Profit margin of } 8.0}{(100 - \text{Gearing of } 60.7)} \times 100\%$$

$$= \frac{8.24}{39.3} \times 100\%$$

$$= 21.0\%$$

Using this formula, we can see that Maykitt & Sellitt delivered a return on equity of 21.0 per cent. Not surprisingly, this is the same result we achieved when preparing the return on equity flowchart for the company in the previous chapter. The real power of this formula lies in the fact that it enables us to readily identify what would happen to return on equity if any of the values of the three performance measures were to alter. However, to fully appreciate the potential applications of this formula, we first need to delve a bit deeper into the logic underpinning it.

It's time for a trip down memory lane – back to those mathematics classes at school. Remember fractions? When looking at fractions you will no doubt have been told the top part of a fraction is called the numerator while the bottom part is called the denominator. In the context of the 4 figure trick, this distinction is particularly pertinent.

The top part of the 4 figure trick formula comprises two elements: asset turnover and profit margin. Performance in both of these areas is reliant on the ability of managers to make sound business decisions. Asset turnover is all about making sure the company invests in the right assets and that those assets are being managed in such a way as to optimize sales. Profit margin is all about effective cost management: ensuring costs are being kept to a minimum as a percentage of sales, but without jeopardizing those sales. So the numerator of the 4 figure trick formula will be determined by the quality of the day-to-day decisions being made by management: poor management decisions will produce a poor numerator, while good management decisions will produce a strong numerator.

The denominator is concerned with how the business is being financed – the gearing. This tends to be a decision made to a large degree by the board of directors. They will decide how much money needs to be raised from shareholders and how much needs to be raised in the form of debt. Also, this tends to be a decision that is only revisited on an occasional basis, so gearing tends to be a far more stable figure than asset turnover and profit margin. This doesn't mean that management can't influence gearing. For example, when managers negotiate credit terms with suppliers, this will affect how the business is being funded.

Return on equity = $\dfrac{\text{Management}}{\text{Finance}}$

THE 4 FIGURE TRICK FORMULA COMBINES TWO ELEMENTS

Here, the 4 figure trick formula can be seen to combine two elements: management and finance. The role of management is to use the finance available to deliver a healthy return on equity. Management's first move in this respect will usually demand the setting of some clear objectives for the year, coupled with a well-defined strategy to achieve them. In other words, management needs to create what is commonly called a budget.

Let's get a popular misconception out of the way. As soon as most managers hear the word 'budget' they think of numbers and detailed reports, but that's not what a budget is at all. A budget is a plan of action: nothing more, nothing less. The numbers aren't the plan: the numbers emerge from the plan. This is a very important point and one that is much misunderstood.

Suppose you're the manager of a training department and you have a plan to run a range of courses and implement a variety of management development initiatives within your business at an estimated total annual cost of $200,000. Then you get to the end of the year and you meet up with the human resources director:

Director	How have we done this year?
You	It's been a great year. We planned to spend $200,000 and that's exactly what we spent.
Director	That's great news! How many courses did you manage to run?
You	Courses? I don't recall running any courses.
Director	Oh! Well what management development initiatives did you manage to implement?
You	Management development? That doesn't ring any bells.
Director	Well, what on earth did you do with the $200,000 then?
You	It was brilliant! We flew the entire training department off to the Caribbean for an all-expenses-paid three-week break. Everyone loved it!

The plan (the budget) was not to spend $200,000. The plan was to run training courses and implement other management development initiatives within the business. An essential part of creating a successful budget is ensuring managers can see through the numbers and have clarity regarding the actions expected of them.

While on the subject of budgeting, we may as well get another popular misconception out of the way. No matter how diligent you are when setting a budget, real life says things will often turn out differently. Not surprisingly, then, as a business progresses through a year, actual performance will often deviate from budgeted performance, and a key role of management is to be able to respond to those deviations. In my experience, it's at this point that managers can get very confused about the role of a budget and the role of a forecast.

Here's a typical scenario which is all too common in business. At the start of the year a budget is agreed and distributed to the relevant managers for them to implement. We're now three months into the year, and both sales and costs are deviating from the budget. Somebody announces, 'The budget is wrong. We need to replace it with a forecast.' Three months further into the year and you'll never guess what's happened – the forecast is wrong. This will need to be replaced by a revised forecast. Things go from bad to worse: three months later the revised forecast turns out to be wrong. This is then replaced by an updated revised forecast.

Not surprisingly, when visiting clients, I'm often asked which is more important as you progress through the year – the budget or the forecast? The first point to note is that a budget is never wrong. That may seem like a very bold, possibly contentious, statement to make, but it's true. All a budget represents is a plan of action to achieve a financial goal. Plans can go awry, but that doesn't invalidate the budget. The role of a budget, apart from representing a plan of action, is to provide a reference point: something to refer to in order to assess how the business is progressing and also to help in making appropriate decisions going forward.

Suppose you plan to meet a friend at a restaurant downtown at 7.30pm, so that's your budgeted time of arrival. You know the restaurant is typically about half an hour's drive from your house, so you set off in your car at 7.00pm. Within minutes you're stuck in the tail end of rush hour traffic. You ring your friend to say you're making slow progress and probably won't get to the restaurant until 8.00pm: that's now your forecasted time of arrival. A little later on, you encounter a road accident, and there's a diversion in place. Time for another call to your friend, during which you very apologetically suggest you may not now arrive until 8.15pm. That's your latest forecasted arrival time. You finally arrive at your destination, but parking proves to be a nightmare and you end up walking into the restaurant at 8.30pm. So here's the key question: which do you regard as more important: the fact you're fifteen minutes later than your latest forecast or that you're one hour later than the original plan? From your friend's perspective, it's the fact you're one hour late that's the reality of the situation. The planned arrival time never changed, and this is the point you should bear in mind when planning to meet someone for dinner again.

If you don't want to be late for dinner in the future, the question you should be asking is: 'Why was I one hour late this time?' The answer to this question suggests that the next time you're meeting for dinner, you should make an allowance for any potential rush-hour traffic; you also need to check to see if there are any diversions in place, and make sure that you leave adequate time for parking. This information will help you to be more reliable and plan more effectively in the future. You can only glean this information by referring back to the original budget (the original plan). The forecasted arrival time is still of use because, even though you're running very late, your friend would still like to be kept updated on your expected time of arrival.

It's much the same in business. A budget is a plan of action to achieve a financial target: that's your destination. You may well deviate from the budget, but understanding why such deviations occur can provide valuable information when it comes to planning for the future. By contrast, a forecast is required to ensure resources are adjusted to meet the more immediate changing needs of the business.

From a planning perspective, this discussion highlights two important financial skill sets that the modern-day manager needs. First, they must have the ability to plan *strategically* – to be able to create achievable long-term business plans. If you want to demotivate management, setting a budget that is viewed as unrealistic at the outset is a very effective way to do it. Second, they must be able to plan *tactically* – being able to respond to short-term deviations from planned performance. This is where the 4 figure trick formula really comes into its own: it enables us to readily assess proposed strategies. Whether we're trying to develop a long-term strategic plan or a short-term tactical plan, the application of the 4 figure trick formula is identical.

So let's look at how this formula can help us plan. The first point to note is that it only comprises three components: gearing, asset turnover and profit margin. In the world of the 4 figure trick, we refer to these as the three 'business drivers'. These are the only three financial levers available to drive any business forward: there isn't anything else. It follows, therefore, that a key element of developing a financially successful strategy is determining what the values should be for these three business drivers.

Asset turnover   Profit margin   Gearing

THERE ARE ONLY THREE LEVERS AVAILABLE TO IMPROVE
FINANCIAL PERFORMANCE

A question I am often asked is, 'What are the recommended values for
the three business drivers within the 4 figure trick formula?' In other
words: what are the recommended values for gearing, asset turnover
and profit margin? The answer is, there aren't any recommended values. What this formula demonstrates is that what counts is how the
three business drivers are combined. For example, if you're running a
business with a low profit margin, you can still deliver a very healthy
return on equity providing you have high gearing and/or asset turnover. Let's look at a couple of examples.

Here are some results you might see when looking at a manufacturer
of luxury goods:

Gearing	55%
Asset turnover	0.65
Profit margin	18%

Putting these figures into the 4 figure trick formula we get:

$$\textbf{Return on equity} = \frac{\text{Asset turnover of 0.65} \times \text{Profit margin of 18}}{(100 - \text{Gearing of 55})} \times 100\%$$

$$= \frac{11.7}{45} \times 100\%$$

$$= 26.0\%$$

Compare this against what you might expect to see for a discount online retailer:

Gearing	60%
Asset turnover	2.60
Profit margin	4%

Putting these figures into the 4 figure trick formula we get:

$$\textbf{Return on equity} = \frac{\text{Asset turnover of 2.60} \times \text{Profit margin of 4}}{(100 - \text{Gearing of 60})} \times 100\%$$

$$= \frac{10.4}{40} \times 100\%$$

$$= 26.0\%$$

Both companies are producing the same return on equity, but are achieving this in very different ways. Starting with the manufacturer of luxury goods, manufacturers typically need to invest significant sums in assets (such as production facilities) in order to trade – which explains the fairly low asset turnover figure. However, because this company manufactures luxury goods, which suggests it has a strong brand, it's able to achieve a reasonably high profit margin. If the business was financed entirely by shareholders (zero gearing), its return on equity would be:

$$\textbf{Return on equity} = \frac{\text{Asset turnover of 0.65} \times \text{Profit margin of 18}}{(100 - \text{Gearing of 0})} \times 100\%$$

$$= \frac{11.7}{100} \times 100\%$$

$$= 11.7\%$$

Without any gearing the company would be producing a return on equity of 11.7 per cent, which is certainly above the 10 per cent minimum we would expect from most companies. However, as can be seen, it's actually producing a very healthy return of 26 per cent and this is being achieved through its 55 per cent gearing. This is a classic example of a company using debt to improve return on equity.

Let's compare this with the discount online retailer. In this instance, the company is trying to attract customers through competitive pricing, which explains why it has a far lower profit margin of just 4 per cent. However, it doesn't need the same size infrastructure as a full-blown manufacturing concern, so it's able to achieve a far higher asset turnover. If this business was financed entirely by shareholders, its return on equity would be:

$$\text{Return on equity} = \frac{\text{Asset turnover of 2.60} \times \text{Profit margin of 4}}{(100 - \text{Gearing of 0})} \times 100\%$$

$$= \frac{10.4}{100} \times 100\%$$

$$= 10.4\%$$

Without any borrowing, this company would be producing 10.4 per cent return on shareholders' funds but, just like the manufacturer of luxury goods, it's managed to significantly improve this rate of return through the use of debt.

As can be seen from both examples, it's impossible to provide recommended values for any of the three business drivers, as it's the combination that ultimately determines the return on equity being achieved. That doesn't mean we're unable to at least get a feel for values, in terms of whether they are perceived as being high or low. Based on my experience over many years, working with a wide variety of companies in a wide variety of industries, the following table provides a rough guide to interpreting the values of the three business drivers.

	Gearing	Asset turnover	Profit margin
Low	Up to 50%	Up to 1.0	Up to 10%
High	Over 50%	Over 1.0	Over 10%

These are broad brush assessments, and don't equate low with bad and high with good. As we've just seen, an online retailer can have a very low profit margin but can still be very successful if it has high asset turnover and a reasonable level of gearing. The aim is to balance all three business drivers to ensure that a healthy return on equity is generated. However, when it comes to developing strategy, it's good to at least have a base position – a starting point.

Referring to the table above suggests an asset turnover of 1.0, coupled with a profit margin of 10 per cent, might be reasonable starting values for these two measures. Turning our attention to gearing, we've already established that the role of debt in business is to enhance the return on equity that can be created by the sound management of asset turnover and profit margin. A logical starting point, then, would be to look at how a business would perform without any debt at all: in other words, with zero gearing. This is all we need in order to create some base values for the 4 figure trick formula.

$$\textbf{Return on equity} = \frac{\text{Asset turnover of } 1.0 \times \text{Profit margin of } 10}{(100 - \text{Gearing of } 0)} \times 100\%$$

$$= 10\%$$

THE BASE FORMULA

You'll note we're starting off with an assumed asset turnover of one. What this says is that the value of the assets will equate to the annual sales figure. Suppose you would like to buy a shop that is achieving annual sales of $500,000. To achieve an asset turnover of one, this says you mustn't pay more than $500,000 for the shop and all its contents. If the value of the assets is greater than the annual sales figure, you're moving into an asset-heavy business; while if the value of the assets is less than the annual sales figure, you're moving into an asset-light business. There's no right or wrong here, as often the asset requirements will be determined by the industry within which you're trading. Car production tends to be asset-heavy. You need a lot of assets in terms of factory space, production equipment and such like before you can even consider trading. By contrast, management consultancies are usually quite asset-light. All you need in order to start up is office space, furniture and some computer equipment.

The next assumption is a profit margin of 10 per cent. If you can make $10 net profit out of every $100 sale, many businesses would agree this is a pretty reasonable position to be in.

The final assumption we're making here is nil gearing, because we want to see how the business would perform without any of the financial risks associated with taking on debt.

What this base formula is telling us is that, if you have a business with an asset turnover of 1.0, a profit margin of 10 per cent and no borrowing, you'll deliver a return on equity of 10 per cent. If you could replicate these figures, you know you have a business that is able to generate an acceptable rate of return. It is, of course, highly unlikely that you'll ever encounter a company that trades on these values, so the challenge for any business is to determine which of these values need to change and by how much. To ascertain this, it's best to split this challenge into two discrete stages. Stage one involves ensuring the business is being managed as effectively as possible, which involves optimizing asset turnover and profit margin. You can then move on to stage two which involves determining how the business is to be financed (determining the most appropriate level of gearing).

In order to deliver a healthy return on equity, a business needs to start off with a well-defined strategy in terms of asset turnover and profit margin. In this respect, most businesses can be divided into one of four broad categories:

1. Low asset turnover + High profit margin
2. High asset turnover + Low profit margin
3. High asset turnover + High profit margin
4. Low asset turnover + Low profit margin.

The objective in each scenario is the same. Ideally, we want to be able to deliver a return on equity of at least 10 per cent without the need to resort to debt. If we can achieve this, the business will be in a powerful position: we'll only be using debt to improve what is already a healthy rate of return.

Let's start with the combination of low asset turnover and high profit margin. If you're in a business which by its very nature is asset-hungry, asset turnover will usually be low. The base formula tells us that, if asset turnover is below one and there is no borrowing in the system, profit margin will need to be in excess of 10 per cent for the business to still deliver a healthy return on equity. We saw how this could work when we looked at our example of the manufacturer of luxury goods which had an asset turnover of 0.65 and a profit margin of 18 per cent. We noted in this instance that, even without any borrowing at all, the company would still deliver a return on equity of 11.7 per cent. This was a classic example of compensating for a low asset turnover with a high profit margin. So if you're in a business with a low asset turnover, you need to ask a question. What can we do to create a high profit margin? In the case of a luxury goods manufacturer, a high margin can be created through strong branding. There are, of course, a variety of other ways to achieve a high margin, such as trading in a niche market where there is minimal competition or maybe using technology to become very cost efficient.

Life becomes a lot easier if you're in a business that has a high asset turnover. Returning to our discount online retailer with an asset turnover of 2.60 we saw that, even with a profit margin of just four per cent, it could still deliver a return on equity of over 10 per cent without the need for any debt at all. This is a classic example of high asset turnover compensating for low profit margin.

In practice, you'll find that many businesses fall into one of the two strategic scenarios we've explored so far. That is to say, many businesses are either low asset turnover combined with high profit margin or high asset turnover combined with low profit margin. In both of these scenarios, gearing is often used to improve what is already a reasonable return on equity.

Wouldn't it be great, though, if a business had high asset turnover and high profit margin? This is less common than the previous two scenarios but it can occur, particularly in service industries where you're paying for a specialized skill. Businesses offering management consultancy, legal services, financial services and such like don't tend to need a lot of assets and they can charge high fees because of the specialist nature of the services they have on offer. This can sometimes give rise to the most fortuitous combination of high asset turnover and high profit margin, resulting in a high return on equity – and that's before any debt is injected into the business.

This leaves us with one scenario: companies with a low asset turnover and a low profit margin. In this situation, where you have a business that is both asset hungry and cost hungry, the business model really does need to be called into question. In such a scenario, the only way to deliver a healthy return on equity would be to raise significant amounts of debt, which in turn would expose the business to significant financial risk if ever there should be a downturn in trading. Although this situation may raise doubts about viability, it's still possible for such a business to exist and indeed trade successfully.

By the way – don't be fooled into thinking that low asset turnover combined with low profit margin is the only circumstance in which a company is unable to deliver a reasonable return on equity (without the need to resort to debt). It's quite possible for a company to have a high profit margin, but to also have such a low asset turnover that it's impossible to deliver a return on equity of 10 per cent without raising at least some debt. The same can be true of a company with a high asset turnover, but with an extremely low profit margin. Why would anybody want to get involved in businesses such as these?

Here's a simple business idea. You want to buy a property with the intention of generating rental income. Suppose the property will cost $250,000 and you expect to generate $20,000 a year in rent. Of course, there will be some ongoing expenses such as insurance, maintenance and so on which you estimate will be approximately $5,000 a year, leaving you with $15,000 profit. For the time being, let's assume the money for the property is coming out of your own pocket. In this situation, gearing would be zero, asset takeover would be 0.08 ($20,000 sales divided by $250,000 assets) and profit margin would be 75 per cent ($15,000 profit as a percentage of $20,000 sales). Putting these figures into the 4 figure trick formula we get:

$$\textbf{Return on equity} = \frac{\begin{array}{c}\text{Asset turnover of } 0.08 \\ \times \text{ Profit margin of } 75\end{array}}{(100 - \text{Gearing of } 0)} \times 100\%$$

$$= \frac{6.0}{100} \times 100\%$$

$$= 6.0\%$$

Without any debt, you're going to generate a return on equity of just 6.0 per cent, but you know there's a good rental market out there and you want to take advantage of it. The only way you can generate a decent rate of return in this situation is to take on some debt. This explains why many property companies have high levels of gearing: they need that debt to deliver a decent return on equity.

As can be seen, the 4 figure trick formula can prove invaluable when setting corporate strategy. It forces us to look at how we intend to combine asset turnover, profit margin and gearing in order to deliver a decent rate of return on shareholders' funds. Even if a business has an evident financial weakness, such as low asset turnover or low profit margin, it can guide us towards opportunities to compensate through the strengthening of the other business drivers. It also provides another significant benefit. It allows us to ask 'what if' questions, which is a critical part of successful business planning.

Let's return to our old friend Maykitt & Sellitt and refresh our minds with a summary of its trading performance during the latest year:

Gearing	60.7%
Asset turnover	1.03
Profit margin	8.0%

Putting these figures into the 4 figure trick formula, we saw how the company had produced a return on equity of 21.0%:

$$\text{Return on equity} = \frac{\begin{array}{c}\text{Asset turnover of 1.03}\\ \times \text{ Profit margin of 8.0}\end{array}}{(100 - \text{Gearing of 60.7})} \times 100\%$$

$$= \frac{8.24}{39.3} \times 100\%$$

$$= 21.0\%$$

A point worth noting is that, without debt, Maykitt & Sellitt would only be delivering a return on equity of just over eight per cent. It's the debt that enables the company to deliver a rate of return of 21.0 per cent. But now imagine that you're part of the senior management team in this company, and you need to decide where to focus management attention going forward.

We're about to be introduced to a powerful analytical tool called sensitivity analysis. This comes in many guises, but they all do the same thing. Sensitivity analysis asks the question 'How sensitive is the outcome to the assumptions being made?' In other words, if you change an assumption, what will that do to the expected result?

Within the 4 figure trick formula, there are only three figures. We're going to look at how sensitive the return on equity of Maykitt & Sellitt is to a change in any of these figures. Here's a challenge. As part of the management team, you're considering three options: should we focus on growing sales, should we focus on being more cost efficient or should we raise more debt? We're going to explore three scenarios:

1. 10 per cent increase in sales
2. 10 per cent improvement in cost efficiency
3. 10 per cent increase in borrowing.

Which will have the most significant impact upon return on equity?

If the value of assets remains unaltered, a 10 per cent increase in sales will result in a 10 per cent increase in asset turnover. Given current asset turnover is 1.03, a 10 per cent increase would mean this increases to approximately 1.13. Let's see what this would do to return on equity, assuming profit margin and gearing remain unaltered:

$$\textbf{Return on equity} = \frac{\begin{array}{c}\text{Asset turnover of 1.13}\\ \times \text{Profit margin of 8.0}\end{array}}{(100 - \text{Gearing of 60.7})} \times 100\%$$

$$= \frac{9.04}{39.3} \times 100\%$$

$$= 23.0\%$$

We now know that a 10 per cent increase in sales would increase return on equity from 21.0 per cent to 23.0 per cent – an increase of two percentage points.

What would be the impact of a 10 per cent improvement in cost efficiency? A profit margin of eight per cent tells us that the company spends $92 out of every $100 sale. A 10 per cent reduction in this cost base would mean reducing spending to $82.80 out of every $100 sale, which would leave a profit margin of 17.2 per cent. Let's see what this would do to return on equity, assuming asset turnover and gearing remain at their original levels:

$$\text{Return on equity} = \frac{\begin{array}{c}\text{Asset turnover of 1.03}\\ \times \text{Profit margin of 17.2}\end{array}}{(100 - \text{Gearing of 60.7})} \times 100\%$$

$$= \frac{17.72}{39.3} \times 100\%$$

$$= 45.1\%$$

A 10 per cent improvement in cost efficiency would result in return on equity leaping from 21 per cent to 45.1 per cent. That's an increase of over 24 percentage points.

The final scenario is to consider a 10 per cent increase in borrowing. With a current gearing of 60.7 per cent, we know the company is borrowing \$60.70 out of every \$100 raised. A 10 per cent increase in this would result in approximately \$66.80 being borrowed out of every \$100 raised. Let's see what this would do to return on equity, assuming asset turnover and profit margin remain at their original levels:

$$\text{Return on equity} = \frac{\begin{array}{c}\text{Asset turnover of 1.03}\\ \times \text{Profit margin of 8.0}\end{array}}{(100 - \text{Gearing of 66.8})} \times 100\%$$

$$= \frac{8.24}{33.2} \times 100\%$$

$$= 24.8\%$$

A 10 per cent increase in borrowing would result in return on equity increasing from 21.0 per cent to 24.8 per cent: an increase of just under four percentage points.

Look at what we've just discovered. Based on three calculations, we've established that Maykitt & Sellitt is extremely sensitive to changes in cost management: far more so than changes in borrowing or indeed changes in sales. I remember once sitting down with the CEO of a multibillion dollar business that was struggling. Performing the same three calculations as above made it quite evident that the key issue was profit margin: even a half per cent increase would have a dramatic impact upon return on equity. The company set a corporate objective for the following year to increase the profit margin by one percentage point. Twelve months later the company had literally doubled its profit; and this was all the result of sitting down with a calculator for a couple of minutes performing just three calculations.

As can be seen, a powerful application of the 4 figure trick formula is to carry out some sensitivity analysis to identify where management can have the greatest impact, which can prove instrumental when formulating strategy. But it doesn't stop there. Having identified the company's greatest sensitivities, the 4 figure trick formula can also help assign what are perceived as attainable values for the three business drivers.

In the case of Maykitt & Sellitt, we've already established that this is a company that's very sensitive to changes in cost management. Of course, improving cost efficiency by 10 per cent is a challenge for even the most cost-focused business. Suppose the company decides to set a less ambitious target and is hoping to improve the profit margin by two percentage points through judicious cost management, from eight to 10 per cent. In addition, to slightly complicate matters, it's seeking some modest improvements elsewhere within the profit-making process. As a result of good asset management and increasing sales, the company would like to see asset turnover increase from 1.03 to 1.05. Finally, management are being pressed to extend payment terms to suppliers, which it is hoped will increase gearing from its current level of 60.7 to 63.0 per cent. What would all this do to return on equity?

$$\text{Return on equity} = \frac{\begin{array}{c}\text{Asset turnover of 1.05} \\ \times \text{ Profit margin of 10}\end{array}}{(100 - \text{Gearing of 63.0})} \times 100\%$$

$$= \frac{10.50}{37.0} \times 100\%$$

$$= 28.4\%$$

As can be seen, combining these three strategic initiatives would increase return on equity from 21.0 to 28.4 per cent: an increase of over seven percentage points.

Being a formula with just three components, it's easy to work through a whole range of combinations of asset turnover, profit margin and gearing to identify the combination that is deemed most appropriate and most achievable. Of course, it's one thing to set a target for any of these three business drivers: it's a very different thing to identify the actions that will be required to achieve it. That forms the subject matter of the next chapter.

CHAPTER 7

Improving Performance

• • •

In the previous chapter we saw how the 4 figure trick formula can be used to identify areas where management action can have significant impact and also identify possible combinations of the three business drivers that will deliver a healthy return on equity. What the formula made very clear is that there are only three possible strategies to increase return on equity: increase asset turnover, increase profit margin and increase gearing. That's it – there are no other strategies available. If you can improve any of these measures without adversely affecting the other two, you know return on equity is improving. The focus in the previous chapter was very much on the figures. In this chapter, we're concerned with the actions required to deliver those figures.

Now comes your first challenge. You want to improve performance of your business and you know there are three levers available to achieve this – but where should you start? When it comes to the 4 figure trick, there's a well defined pecking order. The first one you should always start with is asset turnover. To appreciate why this is the case, reproduced overleaf is the return on equity flowchart we created for Maykitt & Sellitt back in Chapter 5.

We can see in this instance that the asset turnover is 1.03, which means that, from every $100 invested in assets, sales of $103 are being generated. But it's also telling us something else. The significant point to note is that the maximum the company can spend at this stage in the profit-making process is $103 before it moves into a loss-making situation. Suppose the company increases asset turnover to 1.25 where $125 worth of sales are being generated from every $100 invested in assets. Now the company can afford to spend up to $125 before it moves into a loss-making situation. The higher the asset turnover, the less pressure there is on cost management.

GEARING is	60.7%
So for every $100 of funds raised …	↓
Shareholders provide	$39.30
Other sources provide	$60.70
Which is used to finance …	↓
Assets worth	$100
ASSET TURNOVER is	1.03
So every $100 worth of assets generates …	↓
Sales of	$103
PROFIT MARGIN is	8.0%
So sales of $103 generate …	↓
Profit of	$8.24
Which produces …	↓
RETURN ON EQUITY of	21.0%

The need to always address asset turnover first is a point frequently overlooked by many businesses. A prime example of this can be evidenced when companies experience a downturn in sales. In this circumstance, the battle cry is often, 'We have to cut costs!', which is completely the wrong response. The first thing a company should do when trading gets tough is to review its asset base. If it can reduce its asset base, it will be freeing up shareholders' funds. These excess funds could then be returned to shareholders, with the most obvious way of achieving this being through the payment of a dividend. If there are fewer shareholders' funds tied up in the business, the company doesn't need such a high level of profit to provide a decent return to its shareholders. This in turn will take the pressure off sales. What this demonstrates is that, by focusing on asset turnover, it's possible to increase return on equity even when sales are falling. This reinforces the point as to why asset turnover should always be the starting place when reviewing business performance.

It's only when you've convinced yourself that you've optimized asset turnover that you should turn your attention to the profit margin. Profit margin is all about being cost efficient. This means looking for ways to reduce expenditure per $1 sale, but without jeopardizing overall sales performance. If asset turnover is optimized, any reduction in expenditure per $1 sale will improve return on equity.

It's only when you've addressed both asset turnover and profit margin that you should then turn your attention to gearing. As we've already noted, asset turnover and profit margin, combined, form the core day-to-day management of a business. Gearing, by contrast, is all about how you should best finance that business. This involves carefully balancing the potential increase in return on equity that can be achieved through increasing debt against the increased financial risk.

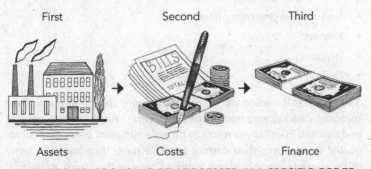

First   Second   Third

Assets   Costs   Finance

BUSINESS ISSUES SHOULD BE ADDRESSED IN A SPECIFIC ORDER

Having identified the specific order in which issues ought to be addressed when it comes to business planning, the next step is to identify the required management actions. Every company operates differently, so it would be impossible to detail specific actions that have universal application. What we can do, though, is identify the questions that need to be asked to identify required actions: these will always be the same.

Let's start our journey with asset turnover. There are two sides to this measure – assets and sales – which implies there must be two ways to address it. The opening move is to examine sales because without sales there is no business. Critical to success is having a well-defined customer value proposition which involves asking several questions. For example, who is our customer? What is our product/service offer? How does our product/service offer satisfy customer needs? What differentiates us from the competition? Why will customers choose us? Combining the answers to these sorts of questions with past trading results, market trends and other relevant indicators will facilitate the creation of a sales plan. Bear in mind that the objective in business isn't to maximize sales; it's to maximize return on equity. So there is one question that should be always in the back of your mind: how will these sales enhance the profitability of the business?

Having estimated future sales, we then need to turn our attention to the assets required to support those sales. Ensuring we have the appropriate assets to support the planned sales is critical to achieving a healthy return on equity. For this purpose, we can divide assets into five broad categories:

- Income-generating fixed assets
- Non-income-generating fixed assets
- Debtors
- Inventory
- Cash.

You may recall – when we studied the balance sheet – that assets are typically divided into two broad categories – fixed (or non-current) and current. Fixed assets refers to things a company owns that are expected to remain in their current form for more than one year. Some of these assets may have been acquired because they form an integral part of the product or service on offer: they directly impact upon income generation. If you were running a taxi business, any vehicles you own would fall into this category. If you were an airline, any aircraft you own would be included here. The asset directly generates income, and these are what we are referring to here as income-generating fixed assets. When we're referring to non-income-generating fixed assets, we're referring to long-term assets that only indirectly impact on income. They have been acquired because they will help generate income, but they don't form an integral part of the product or service being sold. A classic example of this is an office building. Most businesses need offices, but that's not what they're selling to their customers. Every type of fixed asset in a company must fall into one of these categories: it's either an integral part of the product or service on offer, or it isn't.

Now let's consider the other broad category of asset in a business – current assets. These are things a business owns that it intends to consume or turn into something else within a year. You may recall there tend to be three common types of current asset encountered in practice. Debtors refers to monies owed to the business, with such amounts being primarily owed by customers. Another significant form of current asset in some businesses is inventory: maintaining stock to support sales. The final one is cash itself: companies don't acquire cash to admire it; they acquire it to spend it.

Having now divided assets into five broad categories, let's examine the sorts of questions we should be asking when assessing the performance of each one, starting with income-generating fixed assets. The primary issue here is maximizing use of available capacity. Take a passenger aircraft for example. The ideal situation is to have the aircraft with every seat occupied flying 24 hours a day. This may not be practical, but airlines can certainly move in the right direction. They will adopt various techniques, such as differential pricing to maximize the number of seats occupied per flight. They will also try to minimize time on the ground through initiatives such as fast turnaround between arrivals and departures. However, the options don't stop there. They can also look at how the aircraft is configured. For example, maybe there's an opportunity to have more seats through a slight reduction in seat pitch. Regardless of the particular initiative, the objective is to maximize sales per dollar invested, and, in many instances, this equates to maximizing revenue per hour. So, when looking at any income-generating fixed asset, the question that needs to be asked is, 'Are we making the best use of available capacity?'

When it comes to non-income-generating fixed assets, the issue is slightly different. The main issue here is to minimize the investment in these assets without detracting from sales. Take an office building, for example. Is all the space being effectively utilized? Is there excess capacity? Is the office in the right location? It's these sorts of considerations that have resulted in a growing trend to move administrative functions out of expensive city centre sites to cheaper out-of-town locations. The office space may be the same, but the investment in property will have been reduced. Keep in mind when doing this evaluation that sometimes excess capacity is deliberate, with companies arguing they will grow into it over time. Even when presented with this argument, you need to look at the asset objectively and consider whether or not it's appropriate to both current and anticipated needs. So, when it comes to looking at non-income-generating fixed assets, the question that needs to be asked is, 'Are we getting the best return for every $1 invested in these assets?'

Now let's turn our attention to current assets. For many businesses that offer credit terms to their customers, debtors can be a significant issue. In essence, what the company is doing is lending money to its customers. It's saying, 'Don't pay us now, we'll lend you the money for a while'. To all intents and purposes, in part a least, the company is becoming a bank. The objective here is clear: it's to minimize debtors on the balance sheet but without jeopardizing sales. There are various ways this can be achieved. First of all, keep payment terms to a minimum: don't offer 60-day settlement if the customer would be happy to pay within 30. Unfortunately, it doesn't stop there. I have all too often encountered companies with 30-day payment terms, but then they commit the ultimate sin and fail to ensure the terms are being adhered to. As a result, they can end up with customers failing to pay their invoices for months. Tight credit control is the key here. Also, don't do business with customers who are high risk. It's all very well selling something to a customer, but if they end up not paying, it's your business that ends up suffering.

Credit terms are most commonly encountered when running a business-to-business operation, but there is an alternative and it's a practice that's particularly popular when running a business-to-consumer operation – use a third party to provide the finance. When a business accepts payment via systems such as MasterCard or Visa, it's these organizations that are providing the finance. When you make a purchase using a credit card, within the next few days the credit card company will hand over the proceeds due on the sales (subject to a processing fee) to the business concerned. The business has now received payment, and you now owe the credit card company (not the business) for the purchase. Using a third party like this can often free up significant amounts of cash on the balance sheet, which can either be reinvested in assets that will enhance asset turnover or be paid back to the shareholders (maybe in the form of a dividend).

The objective of debtor management, then, is to secure payment as soon as possible after a sale takes place. We've just identified four strategies that can facilitate this: tighter payment terms; tighter credit control; enhanced risk assessment; and using a third-party financier. So, when looking at debtors, the question that needs to be asked is, 'What can we do to minimize the time it takes to collect monies owed from customers?'

Now let's turn our attention to inventory, which is another aspect of financial management that's much misunderstood. In businesses that sell products, a common misconception is that, if you want to achieve a lot of sales, you need a lot of inventory. As we're about to discover, this just isn't true. Here's a quick challenge. Consider two businesses that simply buy and sell pens. They have no other costs whatsoever, and they're rather imaginatively called Company A and Company B. Here are their trading results over the past year:

	COMPANY A $	COMPANY B $
Sales	100,000	200,000
Cost of sales	-60,000	-160,000
PROFIT	40,000	40,000

Based on the information provided, which company do you think is performing better? Most people would probably favour Company A because it's enjoying the higher profit margin. Company A makes 40 per cent profit on its sales while Company B only makes 20 per cent profit on its sales. Let's add some more information:

	COMPANY A $	COMPANY B $
Sales	100,000	200,000
Cost of sales	-60,000	-160,000
PROFIT	40,000	40,000
SHAREHOLDERS' FUNDS	60,000	40,000

Now which company is performing better? Even though sales and costs remain unchanged, it's evident Company B is in fact performing better. Company A is delivering a return on equity of 67 per cent ($40,000 profit on a $60,000 investment), while Company B is delivering a return on equity of 100 per cent ($40,000 profit on a $40,000 investment). This begs a question. Why does Company A need more shareholders' funds than Company B? This goes back to the profit-making process. We know that profit margin is only one stage in what is a three-stage process. Just because one company has a higher profit margin than another company, it doesn't necessarily follow that it's producing a higher return on equity. If neither Company A nor Company B has any debt, the only reason Company A needs more shareholders' funds must be due to its asset turnover.

We're now going to look at the transactions each company indulged in during the year, starting with Company A. At the beginning of the year, the company raised $60,000 from shareholders which it used to buy $60,000 worth of pens. These were subsequently sold over the next 12 months for $100,000. This explains how Company A generated a $40,000 profit from a $60,000 shareholders' investment.

Turning our attention to Company B, this company raised $40,000 from shareholders at the start of the year which it used to buy $40,000 worth of pens. Over the course of the next three months it sold these pens for $50,000. We're three months into the year, and there's now $50,000 physically sitting in the till. To buy more pens, $40,000 is removed from the till, and during the next three months these pens are sold for $50,000. This process repeats itself twice more during the year. This explains how Company B managed to generate $40,000 profit from a $40,000 investment.

The principle we're looking at here is called stockturn, which is an abbreviation for stock turnover. Company A may have the higher profit margin, but over the course of the year it turns its stock over only once. By contrast, Company B has the lower profit margin but it more than compensates for this by turning its stock over four times during the year. We've now identified how Company B managed to deliver the higher return on equity.

The principle of stockturn is at the very heart of inventory management. The objective of stockturn is to keep inventory within the business for the shortest period of time, but without jeopardizing sales. An oft-quoted principle in manufacturing is the just-in-time principle which says inventory should be coming into the business just when you need it. This is an ideal situation, as it results in virtually no cash being tied up in inventory at all. In practice, it is a hard ideal to achieve, but any movement towards that ideal is a move in the right direction. When looking at inventory, the question that should be asked is always the same: 'What can we do to minimize the time inventory resides within the business?'

The only other commonly encountered current asset is cash itself. If you were a shareholder in a company, ideally how much cash would you like to see on the balance sheet? Well, ideally you'd like it to be nil. The worst thing any company can say to its shareholders is, 'We're cash rich. We've got loads of cash!' Why? Because I can put money under a mattress: that's easy. The only reason I would ever invest cash in a business is because I want it working for me. Simply leaving it in a bank account is doing me no favours at all.

This is why in business we talk about cash flow, not cash. Perfect cash management says that, if $25,000 arrives in the bank today, $25,000 should leave the account today and be out there working hard to help the business make profit. Idle cash damages rates of return, so the objective of sound cash management is always to keep cash balances as low as possible, but without impinging on sales performance. If there's excess cash in the business, there are two basic options confronting management: either invest it or return it to shareholders. So, whenever there's spare cash, the question that needs to be asked is, 'Are there profitable opportunities available to invest spare cash into or should we be handing it back to investors?'

What we've now established is that there are five broad classes of asset, each demanding a different approach. The problem is that different classes of asset are more relevant in certain industries than others, and the whole principle underpinning the 4 figure trick is to keep things simple: always focus on the fundamentals. Regardless of the industry, one thing we do know is that it's the assets that are tying up most cash that will have the most significant impact upon return on equity. Logically, then, these are the assets we should be focusing our attention upon. But how can we identify which assets these are? This is where the balance sheet comes to our rescue.

Back in Chapter 3 we looked at the summarized balance sheet of Maykitt & Sellitt where we were told this company had $63 million invested in non-current assets and $88 million invested in current assets. If we were looking at this company's balance sheet in a real-life situation, we would expect to find a lot more detail. Sometimes this additional information is provided on the face of the balance sheet itself. Failing that, you will always find notes accompanying the published accounts, and you may have to refer to these notes to find this additional level of detail. What follows is a more detailed breakdown of the assets within this particular company.

Maykitt & Sellitt Inc. balance sheet (extract) as at 31 December

	Latest year $m	Previous year $m
Non-current assets:		
Land and buildings	21	19
Fixtures, fittings and equipment	23	22
Computer software	9	9
Other non-current assets	10	11
	63	61
Current assets:		
Trade receivables	45	39
Inventories	34	31
Cash and cash equivalents	6	4
Other current assets	3	4
	88	78
TOTAL ASSETS	**151**	**139**

A quick scan of the assets shows us that the class of asset tying up most cash is trade receivables (monies owed by customers), followed by inventories. These are the assets in this company that hold the greatest potential for improving performance. So Maykitt & Sellitt should be focusing a lot more attention on the credit terms it's offering to its customers and how effectively amounts owed are being collected. It also needs to be looking at inventory levels and whether they can be reduced. This doesn't mean attention shouldn't also be directed to the other assets. All we're saying here is that trade receivables and inventory demand attention first.

We're now in a position to develop a structured approach to managing asset turnover. First of all, refer to the balance sheet to identify the classes of asset that are tying up most cash, as these are the assets which provide the greatest potential for improving return on equity. Having established those assets, the next step is to ask the appropriate questions. The following table summarizes the key question that needs to be addressed for each class of asset:

Asset	Question to be addressed
Income-generating fixed assets	Are we making the best use of available capacity?
Non-income-generating fixed assets	Are we getting the best return for every $1 invested in these assets?
Debtors	What can we do to minimize the time it takes to collect monies owed from customers?
Inventory	What can we do to minimize the time inventory resides within the business?
Cash	Are there profitable opportunities available to invest spare cash into or should we be handing it back to investors?

When addressing any of these questions, and this cannot be emphasized enough, it's important to ensure that any proposed action won't end up damaging sales. For example, it's pointless insisting customers pay invoices within seven days if the end result is customers refusing to do any more business with you.

Having addressed asset turnover, it's time to turn our attention to profit margin. We know that reducing any cost as a percentage of sales will improve profit margin and thereby improve return on equity. This is where it's important to make a clear distinction between cost cutting and cost control. Cost cutting means simply reducing costs. If sales fall as a result, return on equity could also fall. Cost control, by contrast, means reducing costs but without impinging on sales. Applying cost control within a business will always result in an improvement in return on equity. So be wary when considering any cost management initiative. Is this effective cost control or is it simply a cost-cutting exercise? Many businesses have suffered because they've failed to appreciate the distinction.

When looking at how to improve profit margin, just as with asset turnover, it's important to focus attention on those areas that can have most impact. In Chapter 3 we looked at a summarized income statement for Maykitt & Sellitt where we observed that in the latest year the company generated $150 million in sales and achieved a net profit of $12 million. Just as in the case of the balance sheet, in practice you will usually get more details provided to you than those that were shown. The most significant area where you can expect to see further detail is within operating expenses, although sometimes this information may be found in the notes to the accounts as opposed to on the face of the income statement itself. Let's look at the sort of detail we might have expected to see in practice for Maykitt & Sellitt.

Maykitt & Sellitt Inc. income statement (detailed) for the year ended 31 December

	Latest year $m	Previous year $m
Revenue	150	133
Cost of sales	-59	-53
GROSS PROFIT	91	80
Selling expenses	-29	-28
General and administrative expenses	-35	-32
Depreciation and amortization	-10	-8
OPERATING PROFIT	17	12
Interest payable	-2	-2
PROFIT BEFORE TAX	15	10
Tax	-3	-2
NET PROFIT	**12**	**8**

You may recall that cost of sales refers to the direct costs incurred to generate the sales during the period. Selling expenses might include costs such as salaries and commissions for sales staff, marketing and so on. General and administrative expenses refers to all those back office functions such as human resources, finance, information technology and so on. However, the line depreciation and amortization requires a bit more explanation. These are two pieces of jargon that are regularly encountered in business, so it's to our benefit that we understand what each of them mean.

You will only encounter the terms depreciation and amortization when a company invests in fixed assets and both of these terms are a direct product of the profit calculation:

Profit = Revenue in a period

LESS The costs incurred to produce that revenue

Suppose a company spends $1 million on a piece of equipment that is expected to last five years. According to the profit calculation, it would not be fair to charge the entire $1 million against the sales arising in the year in which it is bought: the cost ought to be spread over the useful life of the asset. There are various ways this can be done, but by far the most popular method is called the straight-line method which says you spread the cost evenly, which, in this instance, would work out at $200,000 per annum. It's this annual charge that's either called depreciation or amortization.

To understand the distinction between the two terms, you need to appreciate the difference between what are called tangible fixed assets and what are called intangible fixed assets. Tangible fixed assets have a physical form – you can touch them – such as equipment and furniture. Intangible fixed assets have no physical characteristics. For example, when you buy a lease on a property, you don't own the property. What you do own are a set of legal rights that enable you to stay within the property for a defined period of time. Legal rights don't have any physical existence – but you still own them. So a long-term lease on a property would be a classic example of an intangible fixed asset. We use the term 'depreciation' when referring to a tangible fixed asset, and we use the term 'amortization' when referring to an intangible fixed asset. We would therefore talk about the annual depreciation charge when discussing equipment, but would talk about the annual amortization charge when talking about a long-term lease on a property.

We can now turn our attention to the income statement itself. As with the balance sheet, what we're looking for are the big numbers, as these can potentially have the greatest impact. Looking at the performance of Maykitt & Sellitt over the latest year, we can see that cost of sales is the biggest expense at $59 million, followed by general and administrative expenses at $35 million. These should be our first ports of call when looking at ways to improve the profit margin.

Even though looking at the big numbers first seems logical, you might be surprised to hear that many companies fail to do this and, in so failing, simply add to their woes. I was working with a client many years ago where the pressing issue was gross profit. As a percentage of sales it was just too low to sustain the business in the long term. This was a company that urgently needed to redress the balance between cost of sales and revenue. Full credit must be paid to the senior management team because they recognized there was a cost issue and it needed to be addressed. A directive was sent out to all managers to review costs and how they might be reduced. What was the first thing they came up with? Was it costs of production? No. Was it purchase price of raw materials? No. Was it direct labour costs? No. The first thing the management team came up with – and you can't make this sort of stuff up – was to stop providing biscuits at management meetings! Getting embroiled in this sort of trivia is what can lead to the downfall of a business.

The philosophy of the 4 figure trick is to always focus on the big picture. Shareholders really don't care if you have biscuits with your coffee at meetings, but they do care if you fail to deliver a healthy profit. There's an adage sometimes quoted that says, 'A penny saved is a penny earned.' The 4 figure trick would amend this to, 'A penny saved is ridiculous! Save a million dollars – now that's more like it.'

The objective of cost management is very clear: reduce any cost as a percentage of sales, but without jeopardizing sales. Having identified the costs that warrant our attention, what we're now looking for is opportunities to improve cost efficiency. There are a range of questions that can help in this respect. Is this expenditure necessary? Can we get the same product/service for less elsewhere? Would a less expensive product/service serve our needs equally well? Suppose you're looking at expenditure on flights for managers to meet with clients. Is this expenditure necessary? Instead of a face-to-face meeting, would a video call be practical? If a face-to-face is essential, can we get cheaper flights elsewhere? Instead of flying are there alternative, more cost-effective ways of getting to the meeting? Asking such questions before committing to any expenditure can produce significant cost savings.

Sometimes a cost forms part of a process, in which case you should step back from the process. Is there any way the process could be streamlined to make it more efficient? Just because a cost has always been incurred in the past doesn't mean that it has to be incurred in the future. Cost management is all about discipline. It's about ensuring every dollar spent is delivering the maximum benefit for the business.

We've now established a structured approach to managing profit margin. Examine the income statement to identify the biggest costs, as these are the expense items which offer the greatest potential for improving return on equity. Do look at the other costs as well, but make sure it's the big costs you look at first. Having established the costs that demand attention, the next step is to ask the appropriate question. When it comes to cost management, the overriding question is always the same:

Cost	Question to be addressed
All costs	Is there anything we can do to reduce this cost as a percentage of sales, but without damaging overall sales performance?

At this stage, we've optimized asset turnover and we've optimized profit margin. All that's left to be addressed is gearing – how the business should be financed. When looking at the 4 figure trick formula, we noted the primary focus of management is on asset turnover and profit margin: managers are dealing with assets and costs every day. We've already noted that, when it comes to gearing, to a large degree this is determined by the board of directors, but that isn't to say managers can't still have some impact.

Supplier credit can provide a valuable form of finance for a business, and what's particularly pertinent is that it's usually interest free. So, when negotiating with suppliers, there are two issues that are pertinent – the contract price and the payment terms. The longer you can wait until you pay the supplier, the more free finance you're raising for the business, which, in turn, increases the gearing – and we know that increasing gearing can increase return on equity.

This is an opportunity that can easily be overlooked. I've encountered many managers who appreciate that reducing purchase costs can increase rate of return and, as a result, they're prepared to dedicate considerable time and effort to negotiating this part of the contract. What isn't always appreciated is that extending payment terms can also increase rate of return. A word of warning, though: don't try to extend payment terms too far. I was once working with a client who decided to put all suppliers on 120-day payment terms – including me! They soon had to abandon this policy. There are three things that can go awry with such an approach. First of all, the supplier can refuse to supply. Second, the supplier might increase their prices to compensate for the loss of cash flow. Third, and this is particularly pertinent when dealing with smaller suppliers, something more insidious can occur. If you don't pay suppliers for several months, they have no cash coming in to pay their own day-to-day expenses, and that could ultimately result in the demise of their business.

The point to note from this discussion is that extending payment terms with suppliers can improve return on equity – but don't push it too far. It can cause ill will and even result in business failures. So, when it comes to gearing, from a managerial point of view there's only one question to ask:

Source of finance	Question to be addressed
Suppliers	What are the maximum payment terms we can negotiate without increasing costs or compromising the supplier?

The important thing to note about all of the initiatives discussed in this chapter is that you don't have to have visibility of the numbers. I've often encountered managers who say they can't make decisions because they don't have access to the financial information. The 4 figure trick says you can still make commercially sound decisions even if you have no visibility of the numbers.

If you can do anything that improves gearing, asset turnover or profit margin, without adversely affecting any of the other two business drivers, you know you're improving return on equity. To put it another way: if you want to improve performance of a company, you have to have three things at the front of your mind – gearing, asset turnover and profit margin. Always think: funding, assets and costs – they're the only tools you've got. Even if just once a month you had the discipline to take time out and ask the question, 'Is there anything we can do to improve at least one of the three business drivers?', it can lead to an improvement in business performance. Don't underestimate the power of simply asking this question.

One of my past clients became so focused on trying to improve return on equity that they decided to implement a suggestion scheme, encouraging managers to think of new ways to improve financial performance. There was a strong incentive to do this because, under the terms of this scheme, any individual who came up with a suggestion that was subsequently implemented would receive 10 per cent of any financial benefit delivered to the company over the ensuing 12 months. One manager noticed that there was significant duplication elsewhere within the company of a task that was regularly performed within his own department. He gave this some thought and came up with a practical method to remove this duplication, and this one simple suggestion saved the company $5 million in just one year. That was one very happy manager!

CHAPTER 8

The Investors' Perspective

• • •

The primary objective of the 4 figure trick is to make financial management accessible to non-financial managers and to help them readily identify areas where they can enhance performance. Not surprisingly then, up until now, we've been looking at companies from a managerial perspective, exploring how managers can enhance the financial performance of their business. However, to be a fully rounded financially focused manager, it's good to also get a sense of the investor's perspective, and gain an appreciation of how investors think and what motivates them. As we shall discover, having this insight can really help when it comes to planning future business activity.

From our study of the profit-making process, we know that companies need shareholders' funds to finance assets, but now let's consider this scenario from a shareholder's perspective. Why are shareholders prepared to provide the funds in the first place? There are two ways a shareholder can benefit by investing in a potentially profitable company:

1. The value of their shares increases. If this happens, shareholders can (if they so wish) sell them for more than they paid for them. This is called a capital gain.

2. They receive income in the form of dividends. When a company makes a profit, it may elect to pay out some or all of it to the shareholders in the form of a dividend. When this happens, cash is literally paid into their bank accounts.

The combination of these two elements, expressed as a percentage of the share price at the start of the period, is called the total shareholder return (TSR):

$$\text{Total shareholder return} = \frac{\text{(Share price growth + Dividend)}}{\text{Share price at start of period}} \times 100\%$$

Suppose you buy a share for $100, and during the year you receive a dividend of $5, plus the value of the share increases by $15. In this situation you've made a $20 return on a $100 investment. That is to say, you've achieved a total shareholder return of 20 per cent.

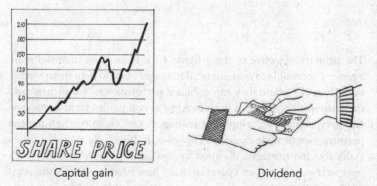

Capital gain   Dividend

THERE ARE TWO WAYS A SHAREHOLDER CAN BENEFIT

Before going any further, we need to be aware that there are two basic types of company:

- Privately owned – companies whose shares are not traded on a recognized stock exchange
- Publicly owned – companies whose shares are traded on a recognized stock exchange.

Most businesses start off as privately owned, with shares being held by just a few people. From a shareholder's perspective, there are two distinct drawbacks with having shares in such a business. First of all, if you want to sell your shares, you can only do this by private treaty: you'll literally have to shop around to find another individual who is prepared to buy them from you. Second, because they're not quoted on a stock exchange, there's no recognized price for the shares, so whatever price is agreed upon will be down to the negotiating skills of the parties involved. In practice, there are two common ways for shareholders in privately owned companies to enjoy a capital gain. One way is when the business is sold as a complete entity to new owners. The other way is by applying for a listing on a recognized stock exchange through a process called an initial public offering (IPO). Various benefits open up when doing this:

- It provides access to millions of potential investors
- It provides a market where investors can readily buy and sell the company's shares
- It enables a market price to be established for the shares (no more private negotiations).

As can be seen, the key distinction between a publicly owned company and a privately owned company is that, in the case of one that is publicly owned, the share price is known, whereas in the case of a privately owned company it can only be estimated. Notwithstanding this, the premise that there are always two potential ways a shareholder can benefit holds true. That is to say, if ever you were tempted to buy shares in a company – it doesn't matter if it's privately owned or publicly owned – you will be attracted by the potential income (the dividends) and the opportunity to ultimately sell your shares for more than you bought them for (the capital gain).

We've already established that, when a company makes a profit, it has two basic options as to what it can do with the money: it can pay it out to shareholders as a dividend or it can reinvest the money back into the business, which will hopefully make the shares more valuable in the future. Dividends are easy to understand: it's literally the money that's paid into your bank account. What's not so readily understandable for many people is how share prices are determined. Suppose you've set up your own business and now you want to sell it. How can you decide what the business is worth?

To understand share valuations, from here on in we're going to look exclusively at publicly owned companies, for the simple reason their share prices are known. It doesn't actually matter if you work for a privately owned or a publicly owned company, understanding share price data can prove to be invaluable when it comes to business planning. For example, suppose you work for a privately owned home construction business. Studying the share prices of your publicly owned counterparts can provide useful information regarding future trading prospects. How is the sector looking overall? Is it buoyant or relatively depressed? This is valuable information. Indeed, understanding share price information for publicly owned companies can be useful for a variety of purposes:

- Assessing the prospects of *a specific company*
- Assessing the prospects of *competitors*
- Assessing the prospects of *an entire industry*.

To understand how to value a company and, by implication, the value of each of its shares, you need to understand a concept known as shareholder value. Directors of companies love to talk about creating shareholder value, where shareholder value can be defined as the value of the shareholders' investment. It's a simple concept. Shareholders invest money in a company, and, logically, they want to see the value of that investment grow. But now we hit a problem. How do you measure the value of the shareholders' investment? In practice, there are two common approaches adopted – book value and market value.

The book value of a company is calculated by adding up everything a company owns (its assets) and deducting everything the company owes (its liabilities), which is exactly what a balance sheet does to work out the value of shareholders' funds. In other words, the book value of a business is simply the value of shareholders' funds as stated on its balance sheet. Suppose a company has assets (such as property, equipment, vehicles and so forth) worth $80 million and liabilities (amounts owed to suppliers, employees, banks, the government and so forth) worth $50 million. This means, in theory at least, the company could close down tomorrow, sell off everything it owns and pay off everything it owes, leaving shareholders with $30 million. This is the book value of the business: it tells us how much money the shareholders currently have physically invested in the company. This is also sometimes called the net asset value (where net assets simply means the value of the assets less any liabilities).

The market value of a company is calculated by taking the current share price and multiplying it by the number of shares in issue. If a company has 10 million shares in issue and the share price is $4.50, the market value would be $45 million. This represents the current price investors would need to pay if they wanted to buy the company in its entirety. This is also sometimes called the market capitalisation. This is where the distinction between a privately owned and a publicly owned company is particularly acute. In the case of a publicly owned company, the share price will be known, so calculating the market value is straightforward. In the case of a privately owned company, the share price needs to be estimated.

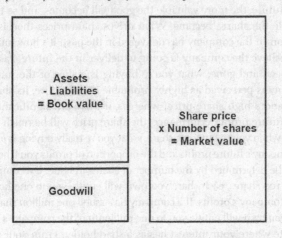

THERE ARE TWO WAYS TO VALUE A COMPANY

The book value is often regarded as an approximation of the breakup value of the business, while the market value represents the value of the business as a going concern. Ideally, every company would like to see its market value exceed its book value, and the difference between these two valuations is called goodwill.

If a company has a book value of $30 million and a market value of $45 million, the goodwill in this situation would be $15 million (literally, the difference between the market value and the book value). This represents the value that has been added to the shareholders' physical investment in the business. So when company directors talk about creating shareholder value, what they're really talking about is creating goodwill. This begs a question – what is goodwill? Based on the figures just quoted, if someone paid $45 million for the company, $30 million is what they're paying for its assets – such as the buildings, equipment, vehicles and so forth. In addition, though, they're paying a $15 million premium for this thing called goodwill. Assuming shareholders are rational, they must be getting something for their money.

Goodwill is commonly portrayed in many guises. It's sometimes said to be the price being paid for the customer base, or the management expertise, or the brand. These can all affect the value of goodwill, but goodwill itself is something very specific – it's the purchase price of future profits. The more profitable we believe a company is going to be in the future, the more valuable the goodwill becomes, and so the more valuable the shares become. What drives share prices then isn't how much profit the company has delivered in the past: it's how much profit we believe the company is going to deliver in the future. Past profits have been and gone; what you're buying is a slice of the future. If a company is perceived as highly profitable in the future, its shares will command a high share price; whereas, if there are significant doubts about future profit performance, the share price will be much lower.

So, when you're buying a share, what you're really buying is a share of the company's future profits and the proportion of profits you'll be entitled to will be determined by the number of shares in issue. If a company has issued 100 shares, each share you own will entitle you to one hundredth of the company's profits. If a company has issued one million shares, each share you own will entitle you to one millionth of the company's profits.

Note where your interest lies as a shareholder. From your perspective, you're not interested in how much profit the company makes overall: what you're interested in is the profit you make on each of your shares. This introduces us to a very important measure of company performance – earnings per share (EPS). It's calculated by taking the company's earnings (which is just another word for net profit) and dividing it by the number of shares in issue:

$$\text{Earnings per share} = \frac{\text{Net profit}}{\text{Number of shares in issue}}$$

Suppose a company makes $60 million profit during a year and there are 20 million shares in issue:

$$\text{Earnings per share} = \frac{\text{Net profit of \$60 million}}{\text{20 million shares in issue}}$$

$$= \$3.00$$

In this example each share is entitled to $3.00 out of the total profit made. From a shareholder's perspective this is far more important than the total profit the company has made. This is because, when profits in a company increase, it doesn't necessarily follow the shareholders will be better off. Suppose a company decides to raise a lot more money from shareholders and in doing so it doubles the number of shares in issue. If profit only goes up 50%, earnings per share will go down, which means the shareholders will be worse off even though profits have increased.

There's another reason for shareholders being obsessed with this figure and that is earnings per share drives share prices. Suppose you're being offered a share that's expected to deliver a $1 profit every year: how much would you be prepared to pay for it? Certainly not $100, because at that price a $1 annual profit only represents a one per cent return on your investment. Even if you paid $50 for it, you would still only be achieving a two per cent return. However, if you were being offered a share for $10, you might now be tempted because a $1 annual profit would provide you with a 10 per cent return on your investment, which is a far more attractive proposition. This is the principle that underpins share valuations. Investors look at the anticipated future earnings per share and, based on that, they'll decide how much they're prepared to pay for the share.

This is a critical point that needs to be appreciated when it comes to share valuations. Share prices aren't determined by how a company is currently performing: they're determined by how we believe the company is going to perform in the future.

In reality, earnings per share and return on equity are just two different ways of looking at the same thing. When shareholders look at earnings per share, all they're saying is, 'On every share we own, we want the company to make us as much profit as possible'. When managers look at return on equity, they're saying, 'In that case, we'll make sure we maximize profit on every dollar invested because, if we're maximizing profit per dollar invested, we must be maximizing profit per share'.

Shareholders focus on
earnings per share

Managers focus on
return on equity

TWO MEASURES OF FINANCIAL PERFORMANCE

What should be evident at this stage is the fact that the focus of managers and investors is somewhat different, and that's because they're focused on two distinct markets. To get a bit technical, managers are focused on what is called the real market, which is all about reported results. Investors, by contrast, are obsessed with what is called the financial market, which is the prospective market. What concerns investors is how they believe the company will fare in the future. The real market is encapsulated in the annual reports of companies, while the financial market is encapsulated in share prices.

So let's imagine that you're considering buying shares in a company. Before you proceed there are two issues that you really need to address:

1. Is the company well managed?

2. Is the share fairly priced?

When it comes to assessing the management of the business, that's where the annual report comes into play. We've already seen how the 4 figure trick enables us, by extracting just four numbers, to construct a return on equity flowchart which can provide valuable insight into how well a company is being managed. However, simply because a company appears to be well managed isn't sufficient reason to buy shares in a company. The price you pay for those shares is critical. Overpaying for shares is equivalent to buying shares in a badly managed business because in both situations you'll achieve poor returns. The real issue here is that, when you're buying shares, what you're really buying is a slice of future profits, and nobody knows for sure what the future holds. This explains why share prices of publicly owned companies can be so volatile. What you need to be convinced of is that the current share price is based on realistic expectations. Buying shares which are based on overly optimistic expectations will inevitably damage your returns.

To assess a share price, you need to look at the anticipated performance of the business and decide whether or not the price fairly reflects that performance. But how can you do this? If you're being offered a share for $50, how can you decide if that is good value or not?

In order to assess a share price, you need to consider carefully what you're buying. We've already noted that when you're buying a share, what you're actually buying is the future earnings (net profit) attributable to that share. We've also noted that when a company is expected to deliver healthy profits in the future, the market value of the company will be significantly above its book (net asset) value. This provides us with two means of assessing share prices:

1. Link the share price to the company's profits.

2. Link the share price to the company's net assets.

The 4 figure trick favours the second approach, but it's the first approach that's by far the most popular: linking the price of a share to the profits of the company. If you decide to invest in shares, particularly those of publicly quoted companies, you will almost inevitably encounter a measure called the P/E ratio (which is an abbreviation for price to earnings ratio). This is by far the most popular measure used to assess share prices, and, as such, you really ought to have some appreciation of what it's all about. It does have its advantages, but it also has some serious drawbacks.

We've already established that what motivates shareholders is earnings per share. The P/E ratio is based on the premise there must be a link between the price people are prepared to pay for a share right now and what they believe the future earnings of that share are going to be. It's calculated by dividing the share price by the latest annual earnings per share:

$$\text{P/E ratio} = \frac{\text{Share price}}{\text{Earnings per share}}$$

Suppose the current share price of a company is $50 and the earnings per share it achieved during the last year was $5:

$$\text{P/E ratio} = \frac{\text{Share price of }\$50}{\text{Earnings per share of }\$5}$$
$$= 10$$

This tells us that shareholders are paying 10 times the current earnings of a share to get their hands on a slice of future profits. In other words, they're paying 10 times current profit. How does this help us assess the share price? When a company has a high P/E ratio, investors are paying far more than current profits to get their hands on a share. Why would they be prepared to do this? They must surely believe earnings per share is going to grow fast in the future. Conversely, if a company has a low P/E ratio, this suggests investors are concerned about future earnings growth.

It's worth noting that interwoven within the P/E ratio is the concept of risk. If a company is perceived as high risk, there will inevitably be concerns about its ability to grow future earnings per share, which will depress its P/E ratio. It follows that, if a company is perceived as low risk, confidence regarding its ability to grow future earnings per share will be greater, thereby increasing its P/E ratio. Notwithstanding this, as a general principle, a high P/E tends to be associated with expectations of robust earnings growth, while a low P/E ratio tends to be associated with anxieties regarding earnings growth.

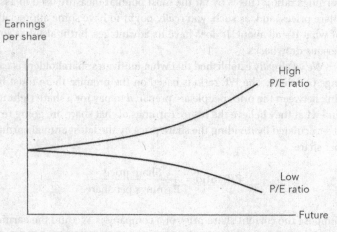

THE P/E RATIO REFLECTS ANTICIPATED FUTURE PROFIT GROWTH

It's important to appreciate that the only thing the P/E ratio is commenting on is anticipated growth in earnings per share, and this is where its limitations lie. Despite its popularity, a P/E ratio tells you nothing about whether or not a company is expected to be successful in the future. Suppose shareholders have physically invested $500 million in a company which last year made a $1 million profit. Forecasted profits over the next three years are $2 million, $4 million and then

$8 million, respectively. If the number of shares are unchanged over this period, this means that shareholders are expecting the company to double its earnings per share every year. In this situation the company will enjoy a high P/E ratio because the growth in earnings is expected to be exceptionally high. However, even if the company makes $8 million in a year, that is still a very poor return on a $500 million investment. Indeed, in practice, when you see companies with very high P/E ratios, it's often because they had a disastrously low profit figure in the previous year – not a great reason to be investing in the business. So the P/E is useful in terms of assessing anticipated growth in profits, but it most certainly doesn't tell you the whole story.

Another limitation of the P/E ratio is that it links the latest reported earnings per share of a company to the share price. What happens if the company made a loss last year? In this situation, there is no P/E ratio. Surely, what would be more useful is a measure that tells us whether or not we expect the company to be a future trading success.

Earlier in this chapter we were introduced to the book value of a company, which refers to the value of shareholders' funds as stated on the balance sheet. We've also noted that return on equity is the measure used to assess how effectively a company is managing to translate these funds into profit. Logically, the higher the return on equity is expected to be in the future, the higher the share price should be. This relationship between the current share price and anticipated future rates of return is encapsulated in a measure known as the price to book ratio (also sometimes referred to as the market to book ratio), which looks at the share price relative to the book value per share:

$$\text{Price to book ratio} = \frac{\text{Share price}}{\text{Book value per share}}$$

This introduces a new piece of jargon – book value per share. This is calculated by simply dividing the book value of the company (as stated on the balance sheet) by the number of shares in issue. Let's revisit the balance sheet of Maykitt & Sellitt introduced in Chapter 3.

Maykitt & Sellitt Inc. balance sheet as at 31 December

	Latest year $m	Previous year $m
Non-current assets	63	61
Current assets	88	78
TOTAL ASSETS	151	139
Current liabilities	-62	-57
Non-current liabilities	-29	-28
NET ASSETS	**60**	**54**
Capital	14	14
Reserves	46	40
SHAREHOLDERS' FUNDS	**60**	**54**

We can see that this company has a book value of $60 million; if you look in the notes to the accounts you'll also be told the number of shares in issue. Let's suppose there are 30 million. In this instance the book value per share would be $2. This tells us that, for every share in issue, there's $2 physically tied up in the business. Another way of interpreting this figure is, in theory at least, if the company closed down tomorrow, shareholders should expect to get back $2 for every share they own. Having identified this figure, the price to book ratio can be readily determined. If the current share price of the company is $3, the price to book ratio would be as follows:

$$\text{Price to book ratio} = \frac{\text{Share price of \$3}}{\text{Book value per share of \$2}}$$

$$= 1.5$$

This tells us that the share price is currently 1.5 times its book value. That is to say, the business (as reflected in the share price) is worth more than its net assets (as reflected in the book value per share). This is good news because it shows the management team have created goodwill – they've added value to the net assets. A far more dangerous position for a company to be in would be where its share price is below the book value per share – that is, the price to book ratio is less than 1.

In this instance the net assets are deemed to be more valuable than the business itself. If management fails to turn this situation around, this could be a precursor to the company being closed down and the assets being sold off (what is sometimes called asset stripping).

So what drives the price to book ratio? In other words, how do shareholders decide whether the shares of a company are worth more or less than their book value? It all comes down to anticipated rate of return. Bear in mind, shareholders have choices. If the general consensus is that a company won't be able to deliver a reasonable return on equity in the future, the share price will be very low; and this will be reflected in a price to book ratio of less than 1. By contrast, if consensus says a company is expected to deliver a very healthy return on equity in the future, the share price will be much higher; and this will be reflected in a price to book ratio of greater than 1.

Let's explore this principle in a bit more depth. To keep things as simple as possible, we're going to confine our attention to anticipated profit over the next year. In practice, we would look at profit performance over several years but, notwithstanding this, the principle remains the same.

Here's a possible scenario. A new company, Grow Fast Inc., has recently raised $100 million to finance assets and achieved this by issuing 10 million shares. This means that the book value of the company is $100 million and the book value per share is $10. The company has subsequently floated its shares on a stock exchange, and you're considering buying shares in it. How much would you be prepared to pay for one of its shares? It's at this stage you need to consider anticipated future rates of return.

Suppose the company is expected to deliver a 10 per cent return on equity over the next year: in other words, it's expected to produce $10 million net profit on the $100 million physically invested in the business. Given there are 10 million shares in issue, the earnings per share works out at $1. So how much would you be prepared to pay for a share that will deliver an annual return of $1? To answer this, you have to take a position regarding what you believe to be a satisfactory rate of return. Suppose shareholders would generally be happy if the company could deliver a 10 per cent rate of return on their investment, and you would also be quite content with this performance. If that was the case, you and your fellow investors would be willing to pay $10 for a share, because at that price the $1 annual profit will be delivering the desired 10 per cent rate of return. You wouldn't want to pay more than this because, even if you paid $10.01, the $1 profit would then represent less than the 10 per cent return you're looking for. In this instance, then, the share price would be set at $10, which would result in a price to book ratio of 1 ($10 share price divided by $10 book value per share). So, the price to book ratio is 1 when a company is expected to deliver a return on equity in the future that is equivalent to the normal rate the investment market would expect.

Let's work through another example. Suppose news breaks that suggests Grow Fast Inc. will deliver an annual profit of $20 million, which, bearing in mind there's $100 million physically invested in the business, equates to a 20 per cent return on equity. This is double the market rate of return. With 10 million shares in issue, earnings per share now works out at $2. In this situation, investors will be prepared to pay $20 per share, because at that price the $2 profit will still deliver their required annual rate of return of 10 per cent. This will result in a price to book ratio of two ($20 share price divided by $10 book value per share).

Here's one final example. News has broken that suggests the company will deliver an annual profit of only $5 million, which equates to a five per cent return on equity. This is half the market rate of return, and earnings per share will only be $0.50. In these circumstances, investors would only be prepared to pay $5 per share if they still want to achieve their 10 per cent rate of return. The price to book ratio will be 0.5 ($5 share price divided by $10 book value per share).

The 4 figure trick is all about delivering a healthy return on equity. What we've now managed to do is take this one step further and establish a link between return on equity and the share price of the company; and the device that has enabled us to achieve this is the price to book ratio. Here's a quick summary of how to interpret this measure:

Price to book ratio	Interpretation
Less than 1	The company is expected to generate a return on equity that is less than the market rate, implying inefficient use of shareholders' funds.
1	The company is expected to generate the market rate of return from shareholders' funds.
More than 1	The company is expected to generate a return on equity that is in excess of the market rate, implying efficient use of shareholders' funds.

The price to book ratio can be seen to be commenting on how effectively a company is expected to manage shareholders' funds in the future: the more effectively it's believed this can be done, the higher the ratio will be and, by implication, the higher the share price will be.

Based on the example we've just worked through, we can see that we would expect the market to book ratio to be 1 when a company is expected to deliver the market rate of return; and we would expect the price to book ratio to be 2 when a company is expected to deliver a return on equity that is double the market rate of return. Using this piece of logic, we would expect the market to book ratio to be 3 when a company is expected to deliver a return on equity in the future that is treble the market rate of return ... and so on.

Applying this logic to Maykitt & Sellitt, its price to book ratio of 1.5 suggests investors are expecting the company to deliver a future rate of return on shareholders' funds that's approximately one and a half times the market rate. So, how does this help us assess whether a share price represents good value or not?

We noted back in Chapter 3 that Maykitt & Sellitt delivered a return on equity of 21 per cent last year; suppose it delivered a return on equity of 19% per cent in the year previous to that. If we expected this sort of performance to continue in the future, we would be expecting the company to be producing approximately 20 per cent return on equity each year. All we now need to do is to determine what, if your forecasts turn out to be right, the market to book ratio for this company ought to be. To do this we need to decide what the market rate of return is. In other words, what's the minimum rate of return that investors would expect from any company? Many studies have been carried out to try to identify the market rate of return, with, not surprisingly, a vast array of conclusions. Several support the commonly quoted management minimum of 10 per cent. That's to say that in the long-term (where we're spanning decades rather than a handful of years), 10% is deemed to be a reasonable rate of return. Studies that focus on more recent stock market performance suggest seven per cent might be more realistic. Ultimately, it's down to you to decide what you perceive to be a reasonable rate of return. The one thing to bear in mind is that nobody knows for sure what the future holds, so there's no clear right or wrong in this situation.

Suppose you decide to stick with 10 per cent. In this case we can readily identify what an appropriate price to book ratio should be for any forecasted return on equity figure. If the market rate of return is 10 per cent:

- A 10 per cent forecasted return on equity would be equivalent to the market rate, resulting in a forecasted price to book ratio of 1.

- A 20 per cent forecasted return on equity would be double the market rate, resulting in a forecasted price to book ratio of 2.

- A 30 per cent forecasted return on equity would be treble the market rate, resulting in a forecasted price to book ratio of 3.

And so on.

So, in the case of Maykitt & Sellitt, where you're expecting a future return on equity of approximately 20 per cent, you'd expect the price to book ratio to be around 2. In fact, at this stage, we've noted it's running at 1.5 which (based on the numbers above) would suggest the company is being priced on the expectation it's only expected to deliver a 15% return on equity. In this situation you may be tempted to conclude the shares are undervalued, so this might be a good time to buy. Of course, if the price to book ratio was 5, you might then feel the shares are overvalued.

Using the price to book ratio like this, as an assessment of current share prices, is by no means a perfect science, but it does at least give you a feel for value. Do bear in mind that all of this analysis and all the conclusions being drawn are based on profit forecasts covering just one year into the future. To ascertain the true value of a share, forecasts ought to cover several years. When this is done, the relationship between return on equity and the price to book ratio isn't quite as clear cut as has so far been made out. However, preparing long-term forecasts is a notoriously difficult thing to do, and inevitably will result in the production of figures which, at their best, will prove to be wildly inaccurate. Consequently, no approach actually exists which can give you a definitive value for a share. The advantage of the approach being advocated here is that it's simple to apply and, although by no means accurate, it can at least give you a sense of whether a share may be currently overvalued or undervalued. For example, if a company is consistently earning 15% return on equity (with no real evidence that suggests this is going to alter in the future) and its price to book ratio is 8, personally I wouldn't invest in it.

It's a great shame that investors didn't pay more attention to this measure back in the late 1990s during what was called the dot com bubble. At the time, I was advising clients to steer well clear of these newly emerging investments. The logic was simple – the price to book ratios were far too high, in some cases running into the hundreds. To justify some of these valuations, companies would need to be delivering a return on equity in excess of 1,000 per cent! It was insanity. Many investors at the time discounted measures such as the price to book ratio, claiming such measures were irrelevant in this new digital age. Regrettably for them, financial reality eventually came back to haunt them: companies failed to deliver the high returns on equity that were anticipated, and fortunes were lost.

Just to give you some idea of how imprecise share valuations can be, some time ago I was called in to work with a major financial services company that was preparing for an initial public offering on the London Stock Exchange. My role was to prepare the 18,000-strong management team for the transition from being a privately owned to a publicly owned company. To assist in the flotation itself, the company also solicited the services of two investment banks. One of their critical roles was to place a valuation on the business. Between them – and bear in mind that these are supposed to be the professionals in this area – they announced that they were pretty certain the business was worth somewhere between $5.5 billion and $10 billion. That's a bit like getting a real estate agent to value your house and being told it's worth somewhere between $330,000 and $600,000!

A point to bear in mind when examining returns on equity and the associated price to book ratios is that these can vary significantly from one company to another, and from one industry to another. Factors such as how asset-intensive the business is and the level of borrowing it undertakes can have a dramatic impact on achievable levels for return on equity and the associated price to book ratio.

The really important point to derive from this discussion is that, in order to achieve a healthy market valuation, a company needs to be able to convince investors that in the future it will deliver a healthy return on equity. In other words, it needs to convince investors it has a management team that knows how to effectively manage the profit-making process.

We've now been introduced to two powerful measures when it comes to assessing corporate performance:

1. Return on equity	This is the rate of return that has been achieved on shareholders' funds in the past, as reflected in the company's annual report.
2. Price to book ratio	This reflects the rate of return that is expected to be achieved on shareholders' funds in the future, as reflected in the company's share price.

We can combine these two concepts into an analytical tool I devised many years ago that I call a *value matrix* – the function of which is to obtain a quick overview of the current trading status of a company. It achieves this by placing the company under consideration into one of four distinct quadrants.

The first step in creating a value matrix is to construct a graph with one axis looking at return on equity achieved in the past and the other axis looking at the price to book ratio (which gives some indication of anticipated return on equity in the future). The next step is to divide return on equity achieved in the past into high and low rates of return. We've already established that any company delivering a return on equity in excess of 10 per cent is generally deemed to be doing well, so this provides a reasonable breakpoint: any rates of return that are in excess of 10 per cent would be deemed high, while anything that is 10 per cent or lower would be deemed low. Similarly, the price to book ratio needs to be divided into what are deemed to be high and low values. We know that any company that has a price to book ratio above 1 is expected to be using shareholders' funds efficiently in the future. This provides the other breakpoint: a price to book ratio above 1 is deemed to be high, while a price to book ratio of 1 or less is deemed to be low. Creating these breakpoints creates four distinct quadrants into which any company can be placed.

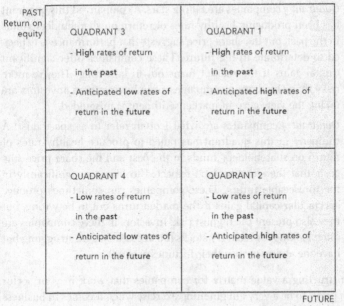

THE VALUE MATRIX

We're now going to explore the significance of each quadrant in turn:

- *Quadrant 1* companies are what I like to call shining stars. A company in this quadrant has been producing healthy rates of return on shareholders' funds in the past and the share price suggests that this will continue in the future. These tend to be well-established, reliable companies and are commonly chosen by investors looking for reasonable future share price growth coupled with (where appropriate) reliable dividends.

- *Quadrant 2* companies can be perceived as rising stars. A company in this quadrant hasn't been producing healthy rates of return on shareholders' funds in the past, but the share price suggests that performance will improve in the future. These tend to be slightly higher-risk companies than those in Quadrant 1, but can offer the opportunity for more significant capital gains if the market has not yet recognized their full potential.

- *Quadrant 3* companies are falling stars. A company in this quadrant has been producing healthy rates of return on shareholders' funds in the past, but the share price suggests that performance is expected to deteriorate in the future. These companies offer significant capital gains if the market turns out to be wrong. They're more risky than Quadrant 2 companies as, in buying them, investors are taking the view current market sentiment is misguided.

- *Quadrant 4* companies are what I often refer to as space dust! A company in this quadrant has failed to produce healthy rates of return on shareholders' funds in the past and the share price suggests that the situation isn't expected to improve significantly in the foreseeable future. These companies can sometimes produce spectacular capital gains if the market turns out to be wrong, but they also present the highest risk. Investors in these companies are often looking for recovery stocks (businesses that are struggling but have the ability to turn their fortunes around).

Constructing a value matrix for companies that work in your sector can prove to be a very enlightening exercise when it comes to business planning. Are most companies concentrated into one quadrant? If so, what does that tell you about future trading prospects? Alternatively, are companies spread across the quadrants? If this should be the case, why the disparity? What can you learn from this analysis that will help your business going forward? Simply looking at other businesses in terms of past trading results and anticipated future trading prospects can be an enlightening exercise and can certainly help management in terms of directing possible future action.

Probably the most important lesson that can be derived from this chapter is that the primary focus of investors is on how businesses are expected to perform in the future. It follows that management should be continually examining their return on equity flowchart and looking for ways to enhance performance. Keep focused on the three business drivers – gearing, asset turnover and profit margin. Have the discipline to regularly ask the question 'Is there anything we can do to improve at least one of the three business drivers?'

CHAPTER 9

Closing Thoughts

• • •

This is a short but important chapter as it brings together everything we've covered in the rest of the book. The one overriding message you should have picked up on is that financial management is not a demonic science. The 4 figure trick says that there are only four numbers that count in any set of financial accounts: sales, net profit, average assets and average shareholders' funds. These four numbers drive every business, regardless of the industry within which it operates. They form the bedrock of the profit-making process – a process which can be broken down into three stages. The first stage involves raising funds to finance assets, the second stage involves using these assets to generate sales, while the third stage involves turning sales into profit. The role of sound financial management is to coordinate all three of these stages to ensure a healthy return on equity is delivered at the end of the day.

Most business failures can be attributed to neglecting or mismanaging at least one aspect of the profit-making process. Probably the most common cause of business failure is focusing far too much attention on the third stage: only looking at sales and costs, while ignoring the first two stages. The 4 figure trick says that successful business management isn't about homing in on what are deemed to be the key issues at the time; it's about being continually aware of the entire profit-making process. To assist in this we were introduced to two powerful analytical tools.

The return on equity flowchart shows us, quite literally, step-by-step, how a company makes profit. Comparing flowcharts from one year to the next can highlight current strengths and weaknesses and can draw attention to important trends. It can also prove to be useful when comparing performance against other companies.

The other analytical tool is the 4 figure trick formula that allows us to ask 'what if' questions, which is a powerful aid when it comes to planning for the future. It enables us to establish, literally in a matter of seconds, how altering any stage within the profit-making process can impact upon return on equity. The really good news is that this can all be done before a decision is ever made.

Another common failing that we've identified is the tendency to get bogged down in detail. The key message here was that details don't kill a business, but fundamentals do. The 4 figure trick says: always keep your eyes on the big picture. A good driver is someone who keeps looking out of the windscreen, not someone who spends most of their time rearranging the contents of the glove compartment!

The 4 figure trick isn't just about understanding a process and focusing on the big picture; it's about a state of mind. Mental attitude can dramatically impact upon performance. Imagine waking up every morning and the first thing you think about is healthy eating. If that's the case, Danish pastries, pancakes with maple syrup along with bacon, sausages and eggs don't get a look in. No – for you, it's freshly squeezed fruit juice, smoothies and granola. Your thoughts are impacting upon your behaviour. Personally, I really enjoy bacon, sausages and eggs with maybe the occasional Danish pastry on the side, but you get the point! Now imagine arriving at work each day focusing on how to manage and improve the profit-making process. Every time you make a decision that could impact upon financial performance you need to be thinking about the three business drivers: gearing, asset turnover and profit margin. That's going to impact upon the decisions you make, and it's this mind-set that's key to managing a successful business.

Sound financial management demands a culture of continual challenge and looking for opportunities to enhance performance. Something I've found that really helps embed the profit-making process in people's minds is to view it pictorially.

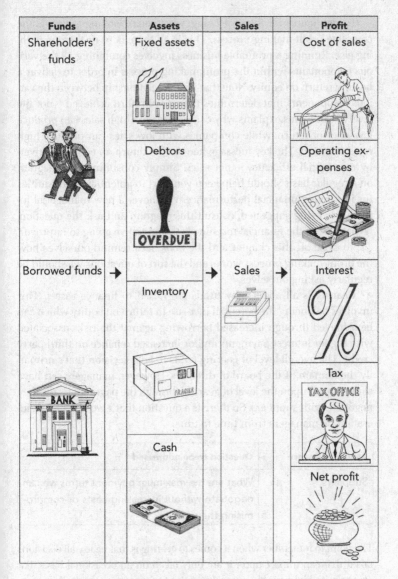

Funds	Assets	Sales	Profit
Shareholders' funds	Fixed assets		Cost of sales
	Debtors		Operating expenses
Borrowed funds →	Inventory →	Sales →	Interest
			Tax
	Cash		Net profit

THE COMPLETE PROFIT-MAKING PROCESS – REVISITED

Forget figures for the time being: what you're looking at here is the complete profit-making process. This is all there is to it; there is nothing else. Running a profitable business involves combining all the various components within the profit-making process in order to deliver a healthy return on equity. Note that it's the relationship between the various components that determines the rate of return achieved – not the level of sales. This explains why companies with high sales can produce low rates of return, while companies with low sales can produce high rates of return. The key message here is that return on equity is driven by managerial efficiency – not sales. Simply consulting this diagram on a regular basis should help keep you alert to potential opportunities for improving financial performance. Whenever a new managerial initiative is being suggested, consult this diagram and ask the question, 'What part of the financial machine is this initiative going to improve?'

To close off this chapter and the book, let's remind ourselves how the profit-making process works and the sort of questions we should be regularly asking ourselves.

Gearing is all about how funds are raised to finance assets. This involves balancing the potential increase in return on equity which can be achieved through increased borrowing against the risks associated with higher interest payments and/or increased reliance on third-party credit. The overall level of gearing tends to be a decision that's primarily the domain of the board of directors. However, managers can have some impact upon the level of gearing through the payment terms they negotiate with suppliers. So there is a question that's worthy of consideration by managers from time to time:

Source of finance	Question to be addressed
Suppliers	What are the maximum payment terms we can negotiate without increasing costs or compromising the supplier?

The point to remember when it comes to gearing is that nearly all decisions taken that can impact upon it are only taken on an occasional basis. For example, it's highly unlikely you'd ever want to contact your suppliers every week requesting a review of their credit terms. Not only might this make you very unpopular, it may well lose you a lot of suppliers at the same time. Once the terms are agreed, that tends to be the end of the matter. Even from a board of directors' perspective, gearing is usually perceived as a strategic issue that merits being revisited only every once in a while.

Asset turnover is a very different matter. Managers deal with assets every day. It's not unusual for managers to walk into their office, go to their desk, switch on their desktop computer, then go to the coffee machine for a coffee and return to their desk ready to start work. Hold on – let's rewind. You enter an office building (that's an asset); you go to your desk (that's an asset); you switch on your desktop computer (that's an asset), and then you go to the coffee machine (that's an asset). You've just encountered four different types of asset and haven't even thought about it. That coffee machine is tying up shareholders' funds, and shareholders want to see a return on those funds. How can you deliver a return? You need sales. The very existence of that coffee machine is putting pressure on the company's sales target.

You should be continually challenging the use of assets, and to this end we noted that assets can be divided into five broad categories, with each category demanding a different question be asked:

Asset	Question to be addressed
Income-generating fixed assets	Are we making the best use of available capacity?
Non-income-generating fixed assets	Are we getting the best return for every $1 invested in these assets?
Debtors	What can we do to minimize the time it takes to collect monies owed from customers?
Inventory	What can we do to minimize the time inventory resides within the business?
Cash	Are there profitable opportunities available to invest spare cash into or should we be handing it back to investors?

Bear in mind that the role of every asset is to help generate sales, whether that be directly or indirectly. If you were running your own business, the only reason you would invest in any asset is because you're convinced that somehow or other it will help generate sales.

The same principle applies when looking at profit margin. Having generated the sales, the role of profit margin management is to keep costs as low as possible to ensure there's still a decent profit left over at the end of the day – every cost needs to be challenged. When it comes to costs, the question that needs to be addressed is always the same:

Cost	Question to be addressed
All costs	Is there anything we can do to reduce this cost as a percentage of sales, but without damaging overall sales performance?

It is this continual review of the profit-making process that will reveal opportunities to improve business performance. Even if you only do this once a month, you may be surprised at the opportunities that reveal themselves. It's worth noting that when asking these questions, you don't need visibility of any figures. Part of the appeal of the 4 figure trick is that it allows us, through its exposition of the profit-making process, to identify what are good financial decisions and what are bad ones. For example, if we can do anything which improves asset productivity, we know we're improving asset turnover, which in turn will improve return on equity. Similarly, if we can reduce any cost as a percentage of sales, without impacting upon overall sales performance, we know we're improving profit margin, which in turn will improve return on equity. A similar argument can be applied when negotiating payment terms with suppliers.

Of course, when you have visibility of figures, that's where the 4 figure trick really comes into its own. Let's just remind ourselves of how to apply the 4 figure trick in practice:

Stage 1.	Extract four figures from the annual accounts:
	• Sales
	• Net profit
	• Average assets
	• Average shareholders' funds.
	The first two figures are sourced from the income statement, while the last two figures are sourced from the balance sheet.

Stage 2. Using these four figures, calculate the three key measures that impact upon financial performance:

- Gearing
- Asset turnover
- Profit margin.

Stage 3. Combine gearing, asset turnover and profit margin to form a powerful analytical tool:

- Return on equity flowchart.

Comparing performance against previous years and other companies can readily highlight those areas where management attention may be required.

This enables us to readily identify those areas within the profit-making process that demand our attention, at which stage we can use the 4 figure trick formula to assess proposed strategies when planning for the future:

$$\text{Return on equity} = \frac{\text{Asset turnover} \times \text{Profit margin}}{(100 - \text{Gearing})} \times 100\%$$

By substituting planned values into the formula, we can readily identify what return on equity would be.

Although the main thrust of this book has been to understand the core principles of sound financial management, focusing primarily on business operations from a managerial perspective, we've also seen how the 4 figure trick can aid prospective investors evaluate the future trading prospects of a company. Investors have two key sources of data: the annual report tells them how the company has done in the past, while share price data tells them how people believe the company will fare in the future. The return on equity flowchart provides a fast and effective means of climbing inside the annual report to ascertain how the company has been managed, while the value matrix provides a fast and effective means of categorizing companies in terms of trading prospects.

In closing, the content of this book has been based on over 30 years' experience working with a wide variety of companies in a wide variety of industries from all over the globe. Much of the work I have done has involved, at some stage, making some form of presentation. One of the greatest rewards I get when doing this is hearing back from delegates about the fact that they're not only now more engaged in the world of financial management – realizing it's not the demonic science it's often made out to be – but that they also feel empowered to make a real difference going forward. Hearing this is what makes a presentation worthwhile. Bizarre as it may sound, the purpose of the 4 figure trick isn't to help managers understand the world of financial management. The 4 figure trick is all about how to make sound business decisions in a time-effective manner. I genuinely hope you too feel more engaged in the world of financial management. I hope the mists have risen and you now feel that you could look at any business and readily identify its strengths and weaknesses. Most importantly, I hope you now feel empowered to make better, faster business decisions that will enhance the financial performance of any business.

Finally, always remember this:

Sales

Net profit

Average assets

Average shareholders' funds

THE 4 FIGURE TRICK SAYS EVERY BUSINESS IS DEFINED BY
JUST FOUR FIGURES

Index